A MYSTICAL INTERPRETATION
OF PROPHETIC TALES
BY AN INDIAN MUSLIM

SHĀH WALĪ ALLĀH'S *TA'WĪL AL-AḤĀDĪTH*

RELIGIOUS TEXTS TRANSLATION SERIES
NISABA

Edited by

M. S. H. G. Heerma van Voss, D. J. Hoens,
J. Knappert, N. R. B. Kramers, B. A. van Proosdij,
J. D. J. Waardenburg

VOLUME TWO

E.J. BRILL — LEIDEN — 1973

A MYSTICAL INTERPRETATION OF PROPHETIC TALES BY AN INDIAN MUSLIM

SHĀH WALĪ ALLĀH'S *TA'WĪL AL-AḤĀDĪTH*

TRANSLATED BY

J. M. S. BALJON

E.J. BRILL — LEIDEN — 1973

NISABA is the name of the Sumerian goddess of vegetation and writing, whose symbol is the calamus (the instrument with which the writing was impressed on the soft clay) on an altar. The Sumerians were the first people to use writing, for keeping accounts and, by extension, inter alia, as a substitute for the oral tradition. For this reason, the goddess has been given pride of place here.

BP
137
.W3213
1973

ISBN 90 04 03833 7

Copyright 1973 by E.J. Brill, Leiden, Netherlands

All rights reserved. No part of this book may be reproduced or translated in any form, by print, photoprint, microfilm, microfiche or any other means without written permission from the publisher.

PRINTED IN BELGIUM

CONTENTS

Preface	VII
Literature	IX
Introduction	1
Adam and Idrīs (Enoch)	4
Noah	11
Hūd and Ṣāliḥ	13
Abraham and his Family	15
Joseph	22
Job	26
Shuʿayb	27
Moses and Aaron	28
Samuel, David, Solomon, Jonah	42
Zachariah, Mary, John the Baptist and Jesus	52
Mohammed	57
Notes	62
Glossary	66

PREFACE

As is stated by the Qur'ān itself (III, 2/3), the divine message sent down to Mohammed confirmed the Jewish revelation put down in the Torah and the Christian revelation made to Jesus in the Gospel. Accordingly, a free use of Biblical material could be, and has been, made when the audience of the Arabian prophet was addressed and admonished. Moreover, since preaching is the endeavour to clarify the conditions of the moment by drawing parallels from sacred stories of the past, it is obvious that in the elucidation of Mohammed's position the Qur'ān displays a certain preference for reports of Biblical messengers of God. The references to those holy men however, are mostly given in a fragmentary form, and have induced Qur'ān commentators and popular preachers to produce supplementary data. In consequence of this a kind of edifying literature came into existence, simply indicated as "Prophetic Tales" (*qiṣaṣ al-anbiyā'*). The immediate function of those stories, as is self-evident, was to stir and satisfy the fancy of the common believer. But to explainers of mystic thought they appeared to be also the material proper for exposing hidden meanings of faith.

The monograph now before us is a fine example of a dissertation on the esoteric background of particular episodes pertaining to the lives of persons who are ranked as prophets by the Muslims. Its full title is *Ta'wīl al-aḥādīth fī rumūz qiṣaṣ al-anbiyā'* ("An Explanation of Significative Events Referred to in the Prophetic Tales"). In fact the events interpreted are mainly haggadic elaborations of Biblical accounts or narratives stemming from New Testament Apocrypha. The author, Shāh Walī Allāh of Delhi (1703-62), was the most outstanding Muslim Indian scholar and mystic of the eighteenth century. This is one of his early writings, dating from approximately the year 1735.

The present text is not a complete version of the *Ta'wīl al-aḥādīth*. Of the first two thirds, up to the records of the characters figuring in the New Testament, only minor parts have been left out in the translation. These omissions are indicated by .... But a select reading is given of the last chapter, which deals with Mohammed, and the framework of which is different from the rest of the book. No sequence of events is observed; instead an evaluation is offered of the career achieved by the Seal of the Prophets.

Wherever Qur'ānic quotations are given or were recognized the numbers of Sūra and verse are subjoined.

For the translation good use could be made of the edition prepared by Mawlānā Ghulām Muṣṭafā al-Qāsimī, and published by the Shāh Walī Allāh Academy in Hyderabad, Sind (1966). This scholar and revered friend also provided a helpful Urdu version of the *Ta'wīl al-aḥādīth*, entitled *Qiṣaṣ-i anbiyā' ke rumūz awr un kī ḥikmatīn* (Hyderabad, 1969).

I am greatly indebted to the Netherlands Organization for Pure Research (Z.W.O.) which enabled me to collect material for my studies of Shāh Walī Allāh's thought in Pakistan and India.

Lastly, I would like to express my gratitude to Mrs. N. Brugman-Begemann for her thorough reading of the translation and for valuable stylistic and editorial emendations.

Leiden, May 1973   J. M. S. BALJON

LITERATURE

Aziz, Ahmad, 'Political and Religious Ideas of Shah Wali-Ullah of Delhi', *Muslim World*, LII, 1, Jan. 1962, pp. 22-30.

Baljon, J. M. S., 'Two Lists of Prophets (A Comparison between Ibn al-Arabī's Fuṣūṣ al-ḥikam and Shāh Walī Allāh al-Dihlawī's Ta'wīl al-aḥādīth)', *Nederlands Theologisch Tijdschrift*, XXI, 2, Dec. 1966, pp. 81-89.

—, 'Prophetology of Shāh Walī Allāh', *Islamic Studies*, IX, 1, March 1970, pp. 69-79.

Bazmee Ansari, A. S., 'al-Dihlawī, Shāh Walī Allāh', *The Encyclopaedia of Islam*, New Edition, Leiden 1965, Vol. II, pp. 254 f.

Fazlur Rahman, 'The Thinker of Crisis: Shah Waliy-Ullah', *Pakistan Quarterly*, VI, 2, Summer 1956, pp. 44-48.

Halepota, A. J., 'Shah Waliyullah and his System', *Systematics*, VI, 2, Sept. 1968, pp. 141-155.

Jalbani, G. N., *Teachings of Shāh Walīullāh of Delhi*, Lahore, 1967.

INTRODUCTION

You should know that whenever God from the Primal Level (where He resides) brings down knowledge upon mankind via the tongue of a human being, it is not communicated by tropes and allusions ... but put in terms of everyday occurrences (*al-tadjawwuz al-ṭabīʿī*). This happens in the same way as when knowledge of what is about to happen is infused in somebody's senses. Then he receives a dream made up of voluntary or compulsory actions and of inanimate or animate bodies somehow indicating what is about to happen ... Similarly, if He wants to point out a truth which is too abstract to be conceived of, God can tell a story or use a figure of speech the tenor of which indicates His purposes, in the manner of a dream notifying an imminent event. ... An example of this is e.g. the statement of God : "Nay, outstretched are both His hands" (Qurʾān, V, 69/64) ... And when God wants to acquaint us with His liberal disposition, He may show in a vision a symbol of liberality like wide open hands ... Hence, I mean by *al-tadjawwuz al-ṭabīʿī* the telling of an occurrence, an arranged event, or the use of a figurative expression which implies a fundamental and spiritual truth. It finds its counterpart in the process of man's unconscious mind (*ṭabīʿa*) when it, receiving vaguely defined information, forms a mental picture of it in a dream.

You should know also that mystic experiences, which come suddenly upon people aspiring after perfection (= prophets), and events arranged in the 'world of pre-figuration' (*ʿālam al-mithāl*) are conducive to their 'perfection' (= becoming a prophet). To those events the same applies as to dreams. Likewise all (other) things that happen in the world are virtually dreams; they are made up of root ideas and of outward shapes.

One of these root ideas is that God wants to direct His worshippers onto a prudent way (*tadbīr*) by means of inspirations, transformations (effected in the properties of elements, as e.g. in the fire which produced a cool effect as soon as Abraham was thrown into it by his opponents) and recommendations ... Accordingly, He selects out of the course of events the one which at that very moment furthers the object of pursuit in the best way ... The event which then appears represents the 'outward shape' and the dream as such, while God's prudent management represents the root idea and the purport of the dream.

To give an example : God wished to appoint a delegate on earth. Consequently, He created Adam. And a supermundane (*mithālī*, i.e. at the level of the *'ālam al-mithāl*) reality, termed as Paradise, enclosed him. Thus he led a paradisical life, but so (by being stationed above the earth) the door to his officiating as a delegate on earth was blocked. Thereupon, in accordance with the purity of his innocent heart, there appeared recommendations pointing out to Adam that he was forbidden to eat from the tree, for this would lead to his expulsion from Paradise. This admonition he gained by dint of a revelation. But the Devil, in conformity with his evil nature, made preparations for infusing diabolic suggestions into Adam's heart. And Adam's nature yielded to the desire of eating from the tree. So he ate, was reproved, and expelled.

All this is a dream and a vision, and its purport is that in this way God wanted Adam to become a delegate on earth and to reach his specific perfection. As for the prohibition of the tree, the infusion of diabolic suggestions, his being reproved and expulsion : all this constitutes a contrivance with the aim that he would gradually leave the supermundane world for the terrestrial world.

Another root idea (in the prophetic stories) is that somebody prepares for developing in his own individuality a certain perfection, such as watching divine mysteries, or establishing a continuous communication with the supreme angels (*al-mala al-aʿlā*), or getting coloured with divine colour ... Accordingly, with the view to effecting such a communication or colouring or getting stripped of depravities, at times an event takes place in his internal perception or in the 'world of prefiguration' (*ʿālam al-mithāl*), depicting one of these processes.

To give an example : in the initial stage of his inner development Mohammed experienced a close communion with the angelic world, bearing resemblance to the supreme angels (*al-mala al-aʿlā*) and being purified from depravities. Thus, gradually his individuality expanded fully. At one time there was a manifestation (of the angelic world) in the form of 'a splitting of the breast',[1] at another time in the form of a discourse by Gabriel sitting between heaven and earth, again another time by the demonstration of his superiority when confronted with other people, and once again on the occasion of his ascent to heaven ...

A third root idea is that the tongue of God appears to be adaptable to different dispositions of an individual. At one time somebody receives a personal message, at another time he may receive a communication for general use ... Thus always that information is obtained which fits a particular situation...

To give an example : in the course of the ascent to heaven (when Mohammed reached the seventh heaven and his Lord) the duty of fifty prayers a day was laid (upon the believers). Then (i.e. when after a successful bargaining by Mohammed on behalf of his community the number of obligatory prayers had been reduced to five) in the end God said : "In front of Me, words cannot be changed" (Qurʾān L, 28/9). Alternately there is mention of five and fifty prayers. In the case of the fifty it relates to a 'tongue of imagery' (since the five are to be considered as worth fifty) and in the case of the five it refers to a 'tongue of factuality' (since this time the human weakness of Mohammed's followers is taken into account) ...

Finally, you should know that when God in His rule of the world displays a breach in the course of nature, He will nevertheless do so within the framework of the customary sequence of natural events, however unstable this may be. ... On this account breaches in the course of nature (i.e. miracles) still have slight natural causes. It is as if these natural causes are always there whenever a decree of God is carried into execution ... Indications pointing to this hidden causality are found in the Qur'ān and the traditions of Mohammed, while clues and imports referring to the same and understandable to mystics and even to any intelligent person occur in (prophetic) tales. The Prophet has declared : "If God has decreed that somebody will die in a particular country, He sees to it that there arises for him a need of going to it". The creation of this need is done for the sake of the maintenance of the order of divine foresight ...

God willing, we shall point out the purport and salient features of every occurrence and in respect of every breach in the course of nature those slight causes. Pay attention to our indications and be alive to them when reading our renderings of tales.

ADAM AND IDRĪS (ENOCH)

At the time when the planets concentrated their spiritual energies on the earth and the archetype (*imām*, i.e. finest example) of the human species requested God to consent to manifest himself in the phenomenal world (*nāsūt*) (with individual forms), and the elements had reached a proportionate composition and yielded a nice kind of clay, God decided under these conditions to create a delegate for Himself on earth, i.e. a species with extensive potentialities for developing his society and economy and with a perfect innate disposition, in which angelic and brutish powers would be united. Out of them divine qualities would arise like spiritual perfection and affection, and it would be proper to give him from above the divine way of religion. And eventually he would become a microcosmos which combines in itself all the realities of the universe on a small scale.

In that place there were angels entitled to learn by inspiration what was impending. They were *'unṣuriyyūn* (i.e. lower angels, composed of 'earthly' elements as distinguished from the *al-mala al-a'lā* who are built of 'celestial' substances). They were agents who through God's inspiration could act upon the elements. By inspiration they learnt that God was about to create a delegate with the following qualifications: he would shed blood and do ill on earth, for which he would suffer punishment in this life and in the life to come. Consequently, they doubted whether it would be wise to create him. For they did not know more than they learnt by inspiration. Therefore, divine wisdom and foresight decided to inform them of what they did not know.

Firstly, by inspiration God indicated to them broadly that for Him there could be good grounds of which they had no knowledge. Secondly, by an event [2] He stated precisely which those good grounds were.

Thus with the leave and will of God there was composed for Adam's creation a proportionate material, being so to say a sample of the whole of the earth with all its different strata.³ For proportionate material — i.e. if touched with heat it becomes hot or if struck with cold it becomes cold — is on account of this assimilative capacity on a par with all the strata. And it was kneaded and became putrid-like; worms arose out of it. Yet its being putrid was 'of a spiritual nature' (*rūḥānī*), and not filthy because it was pushed into contact with a strong force of spiritual entities, as is the case with the putridity of semen in the womb of a woman on which God blows His spirit so that it becomes alive.

In short : since the giving of existence to Adam had for its object the creation of a species, the properties of the species were put into his individuality as if he himself were the species ...; and since there was a concentration of spiritual energies (of the planets at the time of his creation), the properties of those spiritual forces were put into his spirit (*rūḥ*).

And since the contact with his Lord was of a quite recent date (so that he did not yet know God's designs upon him with regard to his delegacy) and since in his constitution the elements and humours were not yet firmly founded (on account of which his body was not fit to lead an earthly existence), he had to lead for some time a paradisical life. Then God planned a contrivance through which the original intention behind the creation of Adam would be disclosed and his innate potentialities would be shown to him. So in him a disposition of an angelic nature was laid, on account of which he was entitled to receive inspirations, as well as a disposition of a bestial nature, which may produce nauseating effects like those resulting from excessive eating. And as soon as both dispositions were untited (in him), Adam possessed intellect more perfected than that of other animals. In so far as this intellect focused particularly on sensuality, passion and the daily necessities, it was inspired to invent wonderful devices (*irti-*

fāqāt) and crafts. And in so far as it focused particularly on angelic qualities, it was inspired with all sorts of worship and purification. Consequently, because of this latter circumstance, he shaped wonderful rites in behalf of his descendants.

Then, in accordance with the before-mentioned three root ideas, some events occurred to him. One of them was that the brisk lower angels (*'unṣuriyyūn*) were commanded to prostrate themselves before him in their true colours, while the angels of the *al-mala al-aʿlā* were commanded to do the same in the shape of any person they pleased, in a way analogous to Gabriel, who took the shape of an inquiring Arab of the desert in the story of his questioning of Mohammed concerning faith, Islam, doing good and whatever he wished to investigate [4] ... Thus, in this distinct way, all the angels together prostrated themselves.

Broadly speaking we can say that their prostration contains a subtle meaning, viz. that by the prayers and pleadings in favour of the sons of Adam the angels are actually worshipping God. Hence Adam and his sons are a *qibla*[5] for their worship. So this subtle meaning was given form by an occurrence : the angels received a revelation which induced them to prostrate themselves.

And in their midst was also Iblīs [proper name of the devil]. By nature he was envious, quarrelsome and arrogant. But until that moment no occasion had occurred through which those blameworthy qualities could have come to light. In his very nature there was a propensity to evil, but the (beneficial) influence of the (other) angels had always dominated over him since he had joined their ranks. At the moment, however, when he was commanded to prostrate himself, he was disobedient to God. Thereupon God cursed him with a severe curse. His sins encompassed him. He became, so to say, metamorphosed onto a deformed shape, and surrendered to evil.

Another event was that the spiritual energies (of the planets) and the imaginative visions of the *al-mala al-aʿlā* encompassed Adam ... Thus he came into Paradise, though he had his actual residence on earth. Hence the laws of Paradise applied to him. But also sensual tendencies were alive in him. So he began to hanker after a female of his kind, and excited he imagined the form of a female. Accordingly, out of his imaginative vision woman came into existence.

Thereupon God provided the contrivance through which the original intention behind the creation of Adam was disclosed. And to the tempers of sensuality and greed He said: "Grasp at what the Devil prompts you to grasp". Thus they did. And out of this arose duplicity because of a mixing up of truth with falsehood and muddling, which bars a proper understanding of truth. One truth was that before entering Paradise Adam had been ordered by the tongue of divine providence: "It is forbidden to eat from the tree; it will occasion expulsion from Paradise, trouble, hunger and thirst". But also another truth had been suggested, viz. that his eating would be the cause of perpetuity, i.e. the continuation of the human species, and the manifestation of God's command and will.

Thus two (inconsistent) pieces of information had reached his subconscious. This made it difficult for Adam. He became confused and perplexed, not knowing what to do. God hints at this confusion and perplexity when He speaks of 'absentmindedness' (cf. Qur'ān, XX, 115/7). Then lust awoke in his breast, so he ate. This was truth mixed up with falsehood ... For, Adam had held that 'perpetuity' meant 'remaining in Paradise' (while in fact the eating resulted in the 'continuation of the human species', since sexuality awoke through it). This mixture of true knowledge with falsehood was a diabolical suggestion, but it was also a (divine) contrivance to realize that which God had willed since eternity. Accordingly, in him biophysical forces came into operation and he became subject to the order of elements and humours. The regions of Paradise receded from him. The angelic régime fell into the background, while the biophysical régime emerged. Then he was told : when biophysical forces will have overpowered your sons and the latter will no longer care for God's inspiration, for God's generosity and wisdom, the necessity will arise of sending to them messengers from among themselves. "And for him who follows the guidance there will be neither fear nor grief. But he who disbelieves will enter Hell" (a nearly literal quotation of Qur'ān, II, 36 f./38 f.), and after that he will be reproved severely ...

Here the parallel of Adam is the man traversing the Ṣūfī Path : devoting himself entirely to God he rises upwards. Then by God ('s power) he is guided to make a tour through the (intermediate) world (lying between the material and the spiritual and divine world). After that he goes downwards (in order to give mankind the benefit of the graces which God has bestowed upon him).

At the moment, however, that his spirit threw off the muddling effects of the biophysical forces there was upon him an effusion of knowledge concerning devices for social and economic progress (*irtifāqāt*) ..., and an effusion of knowledge of articulation and of definition. Thus it fell to him to observe everything.

Then[6] God manifested those items in the '*ālam al-mithāl* in the same manner as He had expounded them in Adam's mind. And God put questions to the angels about these things, their names and their applicability. They, however, could not give an answer, because they did not have the natural ability of making deductions with a reason that is conversant with sensuality, passions and daily needs. Thus the (divine) wisdom (of placing Adam as a delegate on earth) became evident; and by receiving information (from Adam) the angels were favoured with knowledge of things which they had been ignorant of before.

Still another event was that on a certain day Adam, deeply lost in thought, came to know that he himself was the origin of (all) human individuals who might be, according to their different natures, righteous or wicked. (He saw) their (future) forms effusing into the *'ālam al-mithāl*, whereby his being (as the Father of Mankind) was brought to perfection and the fore-ordination of man's existence in the *'ālam al-mithāl* was elucidated. And God asked them: "Am I not your Lord?", whereupon they replied: "Yes!".[7] This answer they made with a tongue of purity, i.e. before they began to stammer by reason of the depravity of their nature. Therefore, because of that event which elucidates their original purity, they can be called to account. Thus like things visualized in dreams that event is a (visualized) form of (man's) original purity. Man's accountability is referred to in information which descends (first) into the intellectual faculties of the *al-mala al-a'lā*, and next into the intellectual faculties of the descendants of Adam.

Finally, there is the event that Adam learnt by inspiration of some activities belonging to the first stage of man's social condition (*irtifāq*). Thus he began with sowing, reaping, threshing, cattle-breeding and the cooking of food. He was given instruction of phenomena of the language, and such like. He took care of procreation, and invented rites for worship.

The position in which Idrīs was placed at first, was that he as a member of Adam's community trod in the latter's steps as regards human learning acquired by inspiration and intuition. In that period he gave his undivided attention to the peculiarities of human life. From this level he advanced to philosophical studies. Consequently, he then concentrated on the particularities of being as it is spread over the whole Universe. Next, he advanced to the centre of *Lāhūt* (= the highest world, where the divine Being is beyond any description or qualification). Then, on a lower level, he occupied himself with the disciplines of natural philosophy, metaphysics, astrology, medicine and applied sciences (*irtifāqāt*). And this was so, because he was somebody who could work with his hands as well as with his power of abstraction (*wahm*) and his reproductive imagination (*khayāl*). Thus many sciences were seen arising from him; and divine providence was operative in them. Hence they kept their value notwithstanding changes of times and customs ... And the religious communities of the Magi and of the pre-Monotheists (*ḥanīfiyya*) came into existence. And the disciplines of medical science, divination and astrology developed well. In those days these disciplines were in a proper condition, whereas nowadays truth is mixed up with falsehood in them. Then, Idrīs made once more an advance. With all his strength he strived after the angelic rank by restraining his passions and by withdrawing from their exigencies. Paradise enclosed him, being lifted to a place on high.

NOAH

It was determinative for Noah's situation that he possessed such strong animal impulses that they were like a veil on the face of the soul, hampering it in attaining its full expansion. The same was the case with most of the people to whom he was sent. Therefore, in order to subdue their animal impulses and to awake their consciousness to the fact that they were human creatures, a body of laws for faith and daily life (*sharī'a*) was made incumbent, obliging them to prayer, fasting and *exercitia spiritualia*. Because of their animal propensities, they did not have the right ability to elicit the subtilties of revealed or acquired wisdom. Nor did knowledge penetrating deeper into these matters descend upon Noah. His mind kept aloof from reproducing and evaluating the objects it perceived, and he did not bother about the knowledge arrived at by Idrīs.

His people were sinning, unbelieving and obstructing social and economic progress (*irtifāqāt*). Their access to God was barred and they deviated from true humanity, though they had a human shape. Consequently, in the *al-mala al-a'lā* wrath was roused against them. And while watching them God pronounced a curse. Vehement was His wrath against them, and He decided on their doom. But all the same warning and the supplying of right guidance remain essential features of God's wisdom, the more so since God has several tongues at His disposal and many modes of expressing his solicitude. And pouring His wrath upon a people in one tongue does not preclude the possibility of His showing solicitude for them in another tongue! And since the total destruction of the species would be a great calamity, God was not very happy with (the idea of) this, nor with having to start again with a new creation (of the species). And inasmuch as an imminent arising of a state of harmony between the celestial and earthly processes of causality (on account of which a devastating flood would rise up) was not in compliance with prudent management, it was required of divine providence (to take counter-measures, i.e.) to provide a contrivance for a continued existence of the stocks of the species. Accordingly,

He inspired (Noah) with the construction of a ship. And of all the species a male and a female representative were assembled in it; and of every tree which does not grow out of itself a seed (was taken into it). Thus God finished His purpose.

And the divine rule looked out for an extraordinary atmospheric event by which He could punish them. When at last the celestial and earthly processes of causality agreed on (producing) a universal flood, at that moment God carried His decision into effect ...

God made Noah a second Adam. And he was the first of (God's) messengers who were sent as servants of divine providence; a function which implies issuing warnings against God's punishments, imposing divine laws, fighting with unbelievers, and taking measures required by divine providence. In (all) these affairs the path of the prophets originates in Noah. His religious community was the first "raised up for men" (cf. Qur'ān III, 106/110) (to guide them). And when some expedients for the permanence of the human species were conveyed to him by inspiration, also some knowledge about devices for social and economic progress (*irtifāqāt*) was added, which he handed down to his sons, as well as some knowledge about temptations—thus he warned his people against the "Deceiver" (Satan)—and some knowledge about monotheism, ways of worship and the subduing of animal impulses under one's angelic nature.

HŪD AND ṢĀLIḤ[8]

These two prophets and their people found themselves in an environment of disbelief and vice. In a similar way as in the story of Noah the *al-mala al-aʻlā* had to pour wrath upon the people and to execute their destruction, whereas the godly man (i.e. the prototype of the human species)—thanks to God's solicitude for him—could warn them and was enabled to find expedients for the deliverance of the believers among them. Accordingly, both prophets became warners and were inspired with expedients for the deliverance of the believers and were given institutions of worship to restrain human passions.

Since the ʿĀdites inhabited al-Aḥqāf[9] and sandy plains so that the atmosphere could fairly soon become dry and warm, the most plausible form of their punishment was a hurricane. In consequence of this, they were deprived of rain for a long period, and their cattle perished. Then they humbled themselves before God; their angelic powers awakened. And they were reprimanded for their evil actions. But even if they would have behaved themselves like beasts, they would not have been punished on a sudden, for angelic solicitude would manifest itself beforehand. Cursed they were, however, as soon as they defied this solicitude. (Now the hour of justice had struck). And when they observed a cloud,[10] i.e. a compact body in the sky, they thought it to be a raincloud. But it was the punishment of God whose speedy coming they had challenged. And it was made 'a roaring blast' (Qurʾān LXIX, 6).

Since the Thamūdites lived in a region of mountains and caves, the most plausible forms of their punishment were earthquakes (cf. Qurʾān VII, 76) and a roaring wind (Qurʾān LIV, 31). Thereupon Ṣāliḥ prayed for their doom. Now that the moment of their doom drew near, he himself was brought into a mood of doom ... And a state which lies between death and sleep descended upon him as it happened to the Seven Sleepers of Ephesus (*ahl al-kahf*).[11] After that he was sent (to them in that condition).

In 'the world of Sovereignty' (*ʿālam al-malakūt*) every wickedness takes the shape of an animal, since wickedness possesses a natural affinity with animals. The last wickedness, however, will take the shape of a man (the Anti-Christ). Then universal doom will be imminent.

At the request of Ṣāliḥ the wickedness of the people appeared in the shape of a she-camel. And when they had killed it, the wickedness (like a soul which is no longer confined to a body) spread on all sides. A hurricane arose. Likewise, when the Anti-Christ will have been killed, wickedness will spread on all sides. And the Great Resurrection will take place. The hurricane was the doom of a single nation, the Resurrection will be universal doom.

ABRAHAM AND HIS FAMILY

The salient feature in Abraham's story is his hankering after the acquisition of the true religion (*fiṭra*) ...

When Abraham became an adult, God gave him wisdom. And he awoke to his natural disposition. Consequently, when he saw the setting of the stars, the moon and sun, he gathered from that clearly that it was his Lord who had created, educated, and guided him; He who is not subjected to the laws of the material and is far superior to what pertains to the human world. A great ecstatic state came over him and Truth shone over him. He became furious about the worship of what was not God. So he broke idols. Thereupon he was thrown into fire. But he was a laudable servant whom God wished to keep alive. Accordingly, God suddenly effused on the matter of fire a cold condition through a wind from intensily cold regions blowing upon it and carrying along an intense cold. Thus it changed the fire. And through the collision of these two a pleasant breeze was brought about (Qur'ān XXXVIII, 97 f.; XXI, 68-70; XXIX, 24).

Next, he felt a tightness in his breast on account of his association with wicked people contending over the true worship of God. Therefore, he emigrated to God, i.e. to a country where he could worship his Lord properly. On the way he met an obstinate tyrant who wanted to harm his wife. So he prayed fervently to God. And by revelation God indicated to the angels that they should enter the body of the tyrant, through the places where air streams into the body. Thus he got a cramp in his hand. After that experience he let her go, and made Hagar[12] a servant to her.

And when Abraham and his wife had grown old and had not received a child, God felt mercy for him and granted him two sons. And God took special care of Abraham since he was a beloved worshipper. And God liked both of them very much. Moreover, mankind was in need of successors of the 'model of religiosity' (i.e. Abraham). And the people most suited for being such a model are they who on account of their character appear to be objects of God's hidden affection. Therefore God deposited in the progeny of Abraham and Sarah prophethood and the Book, and for their posterity He made the call to belief in God's Unity a permanent mission.

And God's intention with regard to the first of the two sons was that He should make him a keeper of His fane (at Mecca), that he should function as an intermediary between mankind and Himself, that he should found a cultic rite by means of which people could come nearer to God, and that he should have progeny with the capacity of establishing a community of Muslims. Now the most natural means to bring him into existence was that Hagar would be put at Abraham's disposal by Sarah. Thus Abraham begot from her Ismāʿīl.

And the most suitable means for achieving Ismāʿīl's arrival in the territory of Mecca was that Sarah would become jealous of Hagar. So she drove Hagar and her son away from her house; and Abraham caused them to live in a desert without herbage. Then at that place God caused a well to gush forth. And through inspiration He indicated the persons destined to settle there. In this way God made His arrangements for the fane. Next, by revelation He indicated to Abraham that he should build the House of God. And by creating clairvoyance in his heart He made him to take up his abode at the House. Then God gave it His blessing, taught him the rites of the Meccan pilgrimage (*ḥadjdj*) and the way how to worship Him in the House, while extending His beneficent power to the piety inherent in him. All this was brought about by an inner revelation which he witnessed in the mirror of his soul. Similarly, God arranged the duties of Ismāʿīl, made him a keeper of His fane, evoked in men a yearning for the *ḥadjdj*, inspired Ismāʿīl to the performance of good deeds, and made him a summoner to the right way of life for his people.

As for the second son : God announced him to Abraham through the intermediary of angels. And through them Sarah's youth was stirred up in her; and she menstruated again. Thus she brought forth Isaac.

And you should know that Abraham, when he dedicated himself entirely to God, was reckoned among the angels living near to God. And through the intermediary of the *al-mala al-aʿlā* he was addressed in a loud voice by the tongue of the (divine) will and election, from an opening for light in the heaven of the 'godly man' (i.e. the prototype of the human species from whom institutions for mankind descend). So he brought to light the falsehood of astrology, Magianism and polytheism.

In this instruction God resorted to a particular contrivance. Since it had turned out that from Magianism syncretism resulted and that through astrology polytheism expanded, the proper way of removing this falsehood for God was to command to follow the true religion (*fiṭra*) and to obey the tongue of the (divine) will (instead of directing oneself to the course of the heavenly bodies). In the beginning of our aeon the things that happened in the world were direct effects of the powers of celestial spheres and elements (*'anāsir*; Gr. *stoicheia*) So Idrīs had spoken of sciences relating thereto. After that, in the Holy Compound (*ḥaẓīra al-quds*) the *al-mala al-a'lā* (being steadily on the increase) crowded together. Well then, each of those supreme angels could function, so to speak, as a secret mechanism in which a potency of the celestial spheres had been laid. Now, if God wanted something to be done, there had to be 'a restraint or a letting loose'[13] (of the causal processes on earth), effected by the *al-mala al-a'lā*. In that way He could have His intention realised. The celestial spheres did no longer keep unlimited command. Hence Abraham came to refute (the importance attributed to) the stars, to teach monotheism, and to call attention to the divine 'irradiation' (*tadjallī*) produced in the Holy Compound.

You should also know that informatory knowledge, which pertains to the *al-mala al-a'lā*, as a rule drips into the souls of the people who have a close affinity with angels; and that it is in the *al-mala al-a'lā* that the divine guidance or curse for men is prepared and prescripts for them are fixed. So it is through the intermediary of the *al-mala al-a'lā* that informatory knowledge comes down to the prophets. And it reaches their ears (in their own tongue) and is adjusted to their personal intellectual capacities.

Finally, you should know that (for the instruction of men)

God has several tongues at His disposal. Thus, when God wanted to explain to Abraham the opportunity of obtaining access to Him by sacrificing to him, He spoke to him with two tongues in order that a great event would occur, that would manifest his making God the exclusive object of his faith and of his obedience while by the same tongue would be indicated that the ransom of the son by the slaughter (of a sacrifice) was a boon worthy of thanks.

To that end the mystery has been disclosed to Abraham that, just as in the case of men, the lives of animals comprise a whole (micro-) cosmos; only in animals things are less specified than in men. And in a vision Abraham was shown that he had to sacrifice his son, whose humanity was of a supreme perfection. A situation analogous to this once concerned our prophet Mohammed when confronted with the obligation of fifty prayers (a day). After that God diminished it to a requirement of five prayers (a day). Then He stated (also) that (notwithstanding this) God actually does not change His word (i.e. the conclusion should not be drawn that God would have recalled a previous decision). Five was the factual number but (as to the reward) it stood for fifty, since (as is said in the traditions) every good work receives a tenfold reward. Consequently, fifty concerned a statement of God, spoken with the tongue of imagery in order to complete a boon and to put obedience to the test.[14]

Similarly, God spoke to Abraham with two tongues :

1. with the tongue of imagery (saying) : "Sacrifice your son", i.e. (sacrifice) a ram without any blemish, which is as precious to its owner as a son to his father. And when he had obeyed (the command of) that tongue, a mighty event[15] happened to him to elucidate his devotion. And in his

book (of good deeds, to be opened on the Day of Judgment) was written that he had sacrificed his son to God. Then, God ransomed him with 'a mighty sacrifice' (Qur'ān XXXVII, 107) to complete the boon and to complete His mercy upon both of them;

2. With the tongue of factuality, saying : "You have accepted your vision as true" (Qur'ān XXXVII, 105), i.e. you have acted on the sense and intention of the vision.[16] By it (in fact) only the sacrifice of a ram was meant.

From the prototype of the human species Abraham received knowledge about social and economic progress (*irtifāqāt*), and knowledge of ethics. Accordingly, he instituted the custom of hospitality and the rights of a wayfarer, specified the imports of a true religion (*fiṭra*), introduced the rite of acquiring access (to God) by a sacrifice, established the basic institutes of Islam, and removed polytheism completely.

To the community of Abraham belonged (also) Lot, who was educated by him and took to heart the lessons he got from him; and this was one of his merits. But in his days there lived people who indulged in impudence and depravity, demoralizing the country, and having sexual intercourse with beasts for the satisfaction of their carnal lusts. Consequently, God's wrath broke over them. And as is in the nature of His wisdom, God would warn them before they would receive their condign punishment. Accordingly, Abraham was ordered by revelation to give warnings, and to do this preferably through somebody of his own community. Hence he sent Lot (to them). And the latter preached, admonished and warned them, but it was of no avail. So the divine wisdom looked out for (a confluence) of celestial and earthly processes of causation that could bring about an atmospheric catastrophe to punish them. And when the doom of God was fixed, angels in a human shape came to Abraham, because he was the man who was actually responsible for giving warnings, and as guests they committed themselves to his leadership. He then offered them food as is due to guests. "And when he saw that their hands touched it not, he was suspicious of them"[17] (Qur'ān XI, 73/70). But as soon as he had understood that they were angels, Abraham and his household were no longer afraid. Joy came over them, and (as an iron mirror is coloured by the colour of the sun through the reflection of light in it) they were coloured by the colour of 'the world of Sovereignty' ('ālam al-malakūt). Therefore (by the angels) the blessing was pronounced on them; "God's mercy and blessing be upon you, oh people of this house" (Qur'ān XI, 76/73).

Angels are part of God's spirit. It is characteristic of the spirit that everything which is touched by it comes to life again and rejuvenesces. Well then, when the angels had pronounced their benediction and exerted all their strength to ameliorate the condition of Sarah, while (on the other hand) the divine mercy looked forward eagerly to the answering of Abraham's prayer, in that situation Sarah recovered her youth. Owing to the annunciation of a son surprise was on her face and in her heart. And by imagining a son in a concrete shape the spirit of the good news circulated in her body. From this circulation blessing resulted, in the same way as a seriously ill person sometimes suddenly recovers on account of joyful tidings; or as people sometimes regain their sexual potency through hearing stories of he-men.

Next, Abraham asked the angels what they purposed to do, and they acquainted him with that. Then they went to the town of Lot and took lodgings at his home. "And his people came rushing on towards him" (Qur'ān XI, 80/78), being up to mischief. But when they came running on and pushed on fighting against Lot, God blinded their eyes. Thereupon He rolled up the earth on the behoof of Lot and his family in such a way that their going away came off smoothly. And they were told not to look back, lest they might find the journey too long. But determination, which so to say serves as a 'form' for the divine spirit, differed among them.[18]

Next, the judgment came down. It consisted of a tremendous earthquake, accompanied with rain, stormy winds, hail-stones, and "blocks of claystone" (Qur'ān XI 84/82).

You should know that punishments coming from celestial regions only occur if planets stand in dreadful conjunctions, and this is the case when rain has been detained in heaven and over a long period a lot of material (like hail and stormwinds) has been accumulated in it, while on earth simultaneously a lot of material (like floods) has been piled up. If the wrath and curse of the *al-mala al-a'lā* concur with this situation, God effuses those processes. And He produces of those materials sometimes earthquakes, a roaring wind, and blocks of claystone, at other times a gale or lightning and a wide-spread fire, or again He makes the earth engulf (people).

JOSEPH

God decreed for Joseph in accordance with the (then existing) celestial processes of causality, trial, affliction and separation from his father, So mighty calamities fell upon him, like becoming the object of his brothers' envy, being thrown into a deep well, being sold, entering into the service of Zulaykha (wife of Potiphar), and captivity till the time of trial was finished. Then God showed His mercy to him, pouring down upon him material and immaterial favours. In what happened to him there were the following provisions of divine providence :

a) His being endowed with intellectual creativity. In a dream the favours were revealed to him which God eventually would bestow on him : people would have to obey him, his parents and brothers would pay him great homage. Jacob explained this dream and expounded the purposes of God. And by his perspicacity in respect of God's secret intentions he understood that Joseph was prepared for the knowledge of *ta'wīl al-aḥādīth*;[19] for, the explanation of dreams and (significative) events can be given by him who disposes of an 'associative perspicacity'. By 'associative perspicacity' I mean the capacity of visualizing basic concepts through images arising from the individual unconscious (*ṭabī'a*), inasmuch as such is postulated by the collective unconscious (*al-ṭabī'a al-kulliyya*) when effusing an archetypal truth into an individual.

b) When his brothers became envious of him and thought of killing him, God put into the mouth of one of them the words : "Do not kill Joseph, but throw him into a deep well! "(Qur'ān XII, 10) ...

c) God provided a contrivance for the deliverance of Joseph : in the mind of traders He put the intention to travel in the direction of the well and to send their drawer of water to the well, where they thought to find water. Consequently the drawer of water discovered Joseph. He kept watchful guard over him, because he had the idea that Joseph would be valuable merchandise. The actual object aimed at by this, however, was a long life for Joseph and the attainment of his true destination.

d) When Potiphar had bought him God put into his mind the idea of recommending him to the care of his wife, and into her mind the intention of meaning well with him and the suggestion of adopting him as a son (Qur'ān XII, 21). The actual object aimed at by this, however, was to procure a permanent abode in Egypt for him ...
e) When the woman fell in love with him and tried to seduce him—and he was a temperamental youth, to that "she got filled with desire for him and he for her" (Qur'ān XXI, 24)—, God showed him a mighty manifestation (of his father who warned him). Accordingly, from his heart an urge of chastity arose. And he disavowed the urge of his nature, though it had a strong appeal ...
f) When Joseph was accused and the good name he had among the people was tarnished, God put into the mouth of a boy wise words by which his innocence was proved.[20]
g) When the wife of Potiphar, after having dressed him daintily, showed him to the ladies in order to refute their criticisms (of herself), they fell in love with him and strove hard to captivate him. In such conditions it was obviously almost impossible for him to remain chaste. So he prayed to his Lord for a way out, if necessary by the imprisonment with which Zulaykha had already threatened him in order to get her way (Qur'ān XII, 32). God answered his prayer. And they thought it proper to clap him into prison, although there were clear indications of his innocence.
h) When the Egyptians were stricken by a terrible drought and they were going to ruin, God in His mercy inspired their king with a device for deliverance. Without Joseph, however, nothing would have come of that inspiration and device. And there would have been no release of Joseph if there had not been that inspiration and an urgent need

of him. Consequently, God stirred up in the hearts of the king and the citizens a need of Joseph, and in the heart of Joseph a need of the king and the citizens, in order that God might accomplish the thing destined to be done ...

i) God made him a vizier. And He made the heart of (the Pharaoh) Rayyān and the hearts of the people submissive to him, and He made this a boon for Joseph as well as for the people.

j) God roused in the hearts of the brothers of Joseph a desire to come to him, so that the afflicted would meet each other. Jacob, being acquainted with monotheism as well as with the cosmic processes, feared the evil eye and enjoined them to caution.[21]

k) When Joseph wanted to detain his brother (Benjamin) in order to come into close contact with him without the knowledge of the other brothers, God thought up a trick for the use of Joseph. And He put into the mouth of his brother the words : "That he in whose camel-pack it (the vizier's cup) shall be found be given up (to you) in satisfaction for it" (Qur'ān XII, 75). They fancied that they would furnish conclusive evidence of their innocence, but unwittingly they were actually playing into the hands of Joseph.

Next, God intimated to Jacob by a revelation in his heart that he would join his sons. Then He completed His favour towards him : while his spirit experienced a radiant joy Jacob recovered his eyesight.[22] And the dream of Joseph came true. Thus (all) these signs (of divine providence) were disclosed to Joseph ... So ponder upon the signs of God, and try to find out in which way God rules His creation.

JOB

The life which Job led was characterised by prosperity, wealth, comfort, religiosity and purity. And he was sent to his people as a prophet, he induced them to the good, kept them from evil, invited them to the religious community of the pre-Monotheists (*ḥanīfs*), and helped the poor and the needy in their distress.

Then the celestial processes conspired in afflicting him, his family and his body. At the same time he enjoyed the solicitude of his Lord, which consisted of grace and serenity of mind. And his very attitude under these circumstances furnished conclusive proof of his obedience to God. And in the account book of his deeds it was recorded, while his Creator gave thanks to him for it.

When his trials had come to an end, God poured down His favour upon him, and disclosed the mercy which had been hidden. And to him was said : "Stamp with your foot. This is cool (water) to wash with and to drink" (Qur'ān XXXVIII, 41/42). As for the stamping on the ground : God's solicitude (actually) made use of earthly processes lest they should lie idle. So He caused a spring to gush forth. A special quality of this spring was that by its water leprosy was cured, as it is a special quality of a sulphur spring that it cures scabies. Thus he took a bath, and drank its water. His epidermis was healed and the germs of disease disappeared. Youth returned to him and his wife. To both of them twice as many children as they had before were born. His sincerity became well-known among his contemporaries and among later generations. And he was blessed with the world's riches like before, yea and more.

One day, when he took a bath, locusts appeared as a mercy

from his Lord, When they settled on his house, they turned into gold. And he tried to catch one of them, which had landed beside the house; for he had decided for himself that if somewhere divine mercy appears, the greatest amount of benefit should be derived from it.[23]

Once he had sworn that he would give his wife a hundred strokes (for some fault, if he recovered). God, however, showed mercy and afforded relief.[24] So instead of keeping his oath to the letter, a formal fulfilment of it was sufficient. A hundred blows carried out to the letter, as is easy to understand, pain horribly, whereas taken in a formal sense they mean only a hundred sham strokes ...

SHU'AYB[25]

Shu'ayb was an upright believer and obedient to his Lord. His fellow citizens worked mischief in the country, infringed upon other people's rights, and drifted into sharp practices. Victims of their injustice called for help in vain. They had completely lost belief in God and the Last Day. As is in the nature of God's wisdom, Shu'ayb was (first) commanded by revelation to warn them of what God could do to them, and to inform them of His (probable) curse of them.

When this warning did not have any effect, the divine wisdom waited until the moment when for a long period rain had been kept back from them, (sufficient) material of the earth had been accumulated and the heat had become unbearable. Then the doom of God did come. A simoom broke on them. Fierce gales set in, accompanied with lightning and thunder. Thus they went to ruin ...

MOSES AND AARON

You should know that the Pharaoh was conceited towards God and His institutes. He pretended to divinity, and made people worship himself. He worked mischief in the country. He subdued the Israelites by killing their (newborn) sons and by despising them, though they were in his country God's chosen people. The latter humbled themselves before God, and sought His aid. Thereupon God wanted to punish the Pharaoh and his people for what they had done, and to bestow blessings upon the oppressed by making them models (for other people) and inheritors (of land). Therefore He fore-ordained the coming into being of a man invested with ample authority, by whose agency one group would come to ruin and the other group would find salvation. And already from his birth up to his becoming an adult Moses participated in the provisions of divine providence ...

One of those provisions was that when the Pharaoh sent midwifes to spy upon the women of the Israelites, He hid Moses from them so that as the result of their inspection they reported: "No pregnancy is there". Next, when he was born a device to rescue him was suggested to his mother by God, (and He advised:) "Give him suck and if you become uneasy about him, cast him into the river; and fear not, neither grieve; surely We will bring him back to you and make him one of the messengers" (Qur'ān XXVIII, 6/7). In this manner it came to pass that she weighed the matter over in her mind, (deciding for herself) that keeping him with her could be an occasion for his ruin, whereas casting him into the river might bring on his rescue; maybe he was the messenger whose coming was announced by the scribes of the Israelites and feared by the Pharaoh. Thus the inspiration dripped down (into her heart) as a premonition, the convincing power of which increased to such an extent that eventually nothing could withhold her from carrying it out. Thereupon God set the waves in motion so that they conveyed the box to the 'people of the Pharaoh'. The latter picked him up; and God excited their interest in him, and the idea occurred to them : "Possibly he will be useful to us, or we may adopt him as a son" (Qur'ān XXVIII, 7 f./8 f.).

It was evident that God had an excellent education in view for Moses and that He wished to make him safe from fear of the Pharoah. Thus is God's mode of proceeding : when He wishes to raise a religious community or a state, an idea is suggested by Him to a shameless man which fits in with his mentality. He then carries it out. Thus, without being aware of it, he accomplishes God's designs. Therefore God's messenger has said : "God indeed has consolidated this religion by a shameless man !"[26]

Next, the mother of Moses felt faint at heart : although she had precisely followed her impulses and had properly responded to the inspiration, yet anxiety came over her that she might have made a mistake and that she should have checked the box before entrusting it to the waves. But God heartened her ... And she said to his sister : "Follow him". And she watched him furtively, while they did not perceive her. Then God wished that she would be delighted and not grieved (Qur'ān XXVIII, 9 f., 12/10 f., 13), that she would take care of him and would give him suck without fear of the Pharaoh. This would be the best thing for Moses in order to strengthen his family-ties to the greatest extent, the most natural way to make him embrace the teachings of pre-Monotheism, and a provision of divine providence for herself, so that she could recognize that the premonition she had received had really been an inspiration from her Lord. Thus she would respond to it and be thankful to God for it, and this would also be the most profitable for a full development of her spiritual life. Accordingly God provided a contrivance : He declared the breasts of the (Egyptian) wet-nurses to be taboo to him (Qur'ān XXVIII, 11/12). Consequently, he refused to suck the breast; all milk he found insipid, so that he made them desperate. Thereupon they brought him to his mother, and her breast he did accept. Thus she was appointed as his wet-nurse.

Next, Moses' knowledge continuously increased in compass and his intelligence in maturity; and his religiousness fully expanded so that when he had reached manhood, God granted him wisdom and knowledge (of faith) (Qur,'ān XXVIII, 13/14). Thus he could explain (divine) laws and was intent upon undergoing the salutary influence of the *al-mala al-aʻlā*. Then God wanted to detach him from the custody of the Pharaoh and to release him from the latter in order that his knowledge (of faith) and integrity of actions should attain a greater perfection. For Moses belonged to the kind of men whose religiousness only comes to full development in an environment of co-religionists; and his growing up in the midst of the culture and milieu of the Pharaoh checked to some extent a healthy development of this. Hence God provided a contrivance which would not be contrary to his rectitude. This was that he intervened between two fighting men with the intention of bringing about a reconciliation. And he was pushed to chastise the wrongdoer. So his hand rushed towards killing. And he asked God's forgiveness as in the conditions of the moment seemed proper to him. And God accepted his repentance. (At a later date) God lifted up the cloud which floated over Moses' heart; (a cloud being there) at the time when he was under the idea that he had sinned. By his killing, however, he actually had been an obedient servant of the divine rule. But in the conditions of the moment it was imperative that he should not understand the secret of this. Accordingly, he became confused and panicked, by reason of the injunctions of the divine law which he knew.

Next, God put into the mouth of him whom Moses had helped and had done a favour, words in which fear for his life were implied. This was a device of God serving as a contrivance to drive Moses out (of the country) and to let him abandon all hope of grace on the part of the Pharaoh. In this manner it came to pass that this person inferred from Moses' words : "You are obviously a provoker" (Qur'ān XXVIII, 17/18) that he desired to thrash him. This story he spread everywhere in the city. The Pharaoh became enraged. Thereupon God put into the mouth of the man who reported this news (to Moses) words urging him to leave (the country) (Qur'ān XXVIII, 19/20).

Next, "when he went into the direction of Midian" (Qur'ān XXVIII, 21/22), without travel requisites, without a female riding camel and without a guide, placing his fate into the hands of God in full confidence, God took care to protect and guide him. And when he arrived at the spring-water of Midian, God provided a contrivance in order to procure for him a settlement in the land of Midian. So He suggested to him to water the cattle of Shu'ayb in a courteous way, while on the other hand He roused in the hearts of Shu'ayb and his two daugthers a feeling for him, because he "was strong and honest" (Qur'ān XXVIII, 26). Thus God accomplished His purpose with regard to both of them according to His will.

Next, He induced Moses to choose the staff which the prophets inherited from each other and which contained beneficent force.[27] Then Moses departed to Egypt, apparently out of love for his people but in reality because of God's determination to effect a prophetic mission. When he had reached the valley of Ṭuwā—a blessed valley in which the spiritual energies of angels were concentrated—God provided a contrivance: Moses stood in need of a fire and of information (about the route), and his wife began to suffer from labour-pains. It had become cold and he had lost his way. And when he reached the lotus tree in that valley, God manifested Himself to Moses in such a wonderful way as He had not done before to anyone else. This entailed that among the *al-mala al-aʿlā* an inner urge was roused to hold a mouth to mouth conversation with Moses. And since Moses was of an unbending, courageous and fervid nature, in his conscious mind suddenly the concept of a fire was formed. Accordingly, God effused the shape of a fire not (made up) of elements and physical processes, but purely of (material coming from) the *ʿālam al-mithāl*. And He spoke to him in that fire by the tongue of the *al-mala al-aʿlā*. Moses became afraid, but God set him at ease. He commanded him to proceed to the Pharaoh, to invite him to the (true) faith. He also showed him the miracle of the staff and the white hand.

As for the essence of both those items (effected by a miracle): just as the *ʿālam al-mithāl* may appear in our world by itself without any connection with physical material like the fire (mentioned above), so it may likewise appear in a physical body—in which case this is regulated and dominated by the *ʿālam al-mithāl*. Thus (as an instance of this second possibility) there was a staff consisting partly of a physical structure, partly of material coming from the *ʿālam al-mithāl*. Its two ramifications were transformed into the jawbones of a serpent. Likewise a flash came over the hand, and it became like a light. At the time of Moses magic was (tantamount to) playing on people's feelings to such an extent that they were induced to fancy in physical bodies the existence of in reality non-existent qualities and characteristics. And it was by a kind of super-magic[28] that truth manifested itself ...

On that day ('of the burning bush') God summed up all the provisions of divine providence he had been favoured with, as (e.g.) at the time when He granted revelations to his mother, when He made him an object of love (cf. Qur'ān XX, 38f), and so on down to the present day. God apprised him of the fundamentals of the practice of religion, and of the method of polemizing with the Pharaoh. And Moses asked all sorts of questions, as e.g. about the unbuttoning of his tongue. God appointed his brother to be his vizier (Qur'ān XVX, 37/5). Thus He gratified all his wishes.

When Moses started his dispute with the Pharaoh, God had made (several) provisions of His providence in behalf of him, on account of his being an object of God's love and pleasure, as well as (several) Plagues in consequence of the divine curse of the Pharaoh and his people ...

One of those provisions was that when the Pharaoh (and his clan) wanted to kill Moses, God sent a believing man of Pharaoh's family to admonish them, so that he would deter them from their purpose and raise hesitation about their desision (cf. Qur'ān XL, 29 ff./28 ff.). Thereupon He put into their minds the thought to adjourn the affair of Moses and to try to oppose him through the magicians (cf. Qur'ān XXVI, 35 f/36 f.), presuming that in a matter of this kind they were superior. In fact, however, this was a (divine) contrivance to demonstrate Moses' superiority and his more effective miracles ...

Another of those provisions was that God afflicted them "with nine clear signs" (Qur'ān XVII, 103/101). Whenever

Moses prayed to put an end to a plague, God did so; and whenever he prayed to bring one down, God did accordingly.

Again another of those provisions was that God ordered Moses to make for the sea. Then, "the Pharaoh followed them with his armies" (Qur'ān XX, 81/78). And when they had reached the sea, God gave a fierce wind mastery over it. It cleaved the sea and made a part of it dry; and it disposed of the sea as freely as it does with parts of the earth when it has become a cyclone.[29] Thus God rescued the Israelites and brought about the ruin of the Pharaoh and his armies.

Next, when the Israelites were proceeding to Jerusalem, they passed "a people who gave themselves up to idols" (Qur'ān VII, 134/138). Some insolent fellows (among the Israelites), in whose hearts the fervour of faith had not entered, said (to Moses): "Make us a god, as they have gods!" They said so, because in their nature there was no inner urge left to turn their faces to 'the World of divine Omnipotence' (*ālam al-djabarūt*). And when Moses had given them a smart lesson, they asked for an outward appearance of the divine world so that by this means they could turn their faces to 'the World of divine Omnipotence'. Thereupon Moses informed them of the truth and disproved their claims. Only by great effort were they prevented from (their intention). And having no answer ready they became silent. But the Samaritan[30] comprehended them, and did with them what he liked.

Next, God promised Moses to take him into His confidence in a blessed site, and to grant him tablets and laws. The special quality of that site was that spiritual energies of angels were concentrated there, and because of that concentration all perceptible contours were blotted out (by the flood of light produced). Moses himself was sitting there in strict isolation, devoting himself entirely to the remembrance of God; and he became like an angel. When he saw the place in which God manifested Himself, he was seized with awe and experienced a strange delight. Then God gave Moses the tablets, in which (words of) divine guidance and mercy were engraved, i.e. admonishments, lessons of history, and God's attributes and outstanding deeds. The material of the tablets consisted of paradisiac emerald, i.e. matter which resembled emerals and which God had created directly—without a secondary means—through His word : Be !

After (the departure of) Moses the Samaritan led the Israelites astray by casting into the molten calf a handful of dust (taken) from a footprint of Gabriel (cf. Qur'ān XX, 96); a peculiarity of the latter's footsteps is that they give life to whatever they touch.

That (episode) was in essence a mercy for the righteous Israelites (since, as will be presently explained, by it they were purged from impious fellow citizens), and a way to rehabilitation for the insolent Israelites, for which at that time they were prepared. For it was like this : among the Israelites there were people who were devils by nature and inclined to worship other objects than God. And from time to time their impiety became extravagant. Therefore, God wanted to purge the Israelites from them. Among them there were also people who, so long as they would continue to exist in this life, would never come to a sound faith, their inferior nature forming a stumbling-block. Hence the best thing for them was that they would be killed in a state of obedience,[31] in order that in the interval between death and resurrection their souls could make still greater progress.

Thereupon, the Samaritan was called to account. Moses exposed his falsehood and invoked evil upon him.

One of the provisions of divine providence for Moses was

that, when people taunted him with a swollen testicle—since he used to cover his genitals when washing himself they had got the idea that he wanted to hide a physical defect—, "God cleared him from what they said. And of God he was highly esteemed" (Qur'ān XXXIII, 69); He did not like anybody taunting him. In this way it came to pass: one day when passing water Moses wanted to wash himself. To this end he laid his garments on a stone. Then that stone rolled away on the ground, so that the Israelites saw Moses (who ran after it) naked, and they could establish that he had no swollen testicle.

And when Moses noticed that (God's) providence was concentrated upon him in a most perfect way and that his potentialities had become like those of the *al-mala al-a'lā*, he asked God that he might see Him from face to face, i.e. that he might see His light, for the sake of which the Universal Soul (*al-nafs al-kulliyya*) had to enclose a piece of material (originated) from the *'ālam al-mithāl* and had to make it a luminous body which would represent the level of Moses' knowledge of his Lord ... Such is the meaning implied in (Moses' statement to be found in) God's Word: "Enable me to look upon Thee" (Qur'ān VII, 139/143).

The possibility of looking upon God, however, depended entirely on an appropriate insight on the part of Moses into the ways of acting of the Primordial Soul (*al-nafs al-ūlā*: the first emanation of God) when it is anxious to guide someone of (God's) beloved, as was also the case with Moses at the moment he yearned after the fire (of the burning bush). But at that time, i.e. in the beginning of his appearance (as a prophet), only the possibility of concentrating his being on God was offered to him, and he did not (yet) possess the possibility of administering the creation in conjunction with God. And at that time God endowed him with a theophany of fire, bearing his fervid nature in mind. But it did not burn him. If (on the other hand) God would have granted a theophany of burning fire just now (when Moses on the mountain had become like an angel and possessed much greater potentialities), it would have burned down everything in its path; for that theophany would have had the shape of Moses as reflected in God's mirror. So Moses should have understood that when God reveals Himself by means of an object He will do so only in the shape it has in His mirror. Then that object adopts a form of the divine in accordance with its disposition. Far be it from a prophet that he would be ignorant of such affairs! Still Moses did not perceive that if at that very moment God would reveal Himself by means of the shape he himself had (in God's mirror), his body would be destroyed. However, the divine mercy for mankind intended his staying alive. So God had mercy with him. "And when God manifested Himself to the mountain, He turned it into dust and Moses fell down thunderstruck. And when he regained consciousness (Qur'ān VII, 139 f./143 f.), the subtle point (which he had not understood) was disclosed to him. And he promised God not to ask henceforth for anything which would not suit his disposition.

Among the people of Moses there arose a similar desire as had been cherished by Moses, because from him a craving for manifestations of the Universal Soul (*al-nafs al-kulliyya*) was reflected in their hearts. Consequently, God revealed Himself in the shape of a lightning and caused them to perish. Thereupon, out of mercy for Moses He resuscitated them (Qur'ān II, 52 f./55 f.).

Next, He commanded them to settle in the Holy Land, and bestowed it on them as a fief. It was ruled by a people of barbarians. Therefore, they were called up to the Holy War and received a promise of divine support. And Moses set over every tribe a leader in order to remain informed of them, to pass on through them commands and prohibitions, and to categorize through them the people by ethical standards. And he sent those leaders as spies to the barbarians. Two of them returned with encouraging reports, the others with defeatist information. Accordingly, God showed His mercy to those two men and made of them faithful witnesses of truth and delegates, whereas He put His wrath on the others and caused them to perish.

When those contradictory reports came in, the Israelites proved too cowardly to fight the barbarians. God reproved them, (and gave them notice) that for many years to come He would let them wander about in the desert (Qur'ān V, 29/26). Thus their provisions were exhausted. Thereupon Moses prayed fervently. And God gave them manna and quails to eat by restraining and expanding processes of causality. And to protect them against the sun He made a dense cloud as a shade, and to serve as torches and lights He made for them a pillar of fire. And He extended His beneficent power to their clothes, for they became neither dirty nor worn ...

Regularly Moses received inspirations in his mind. Thus once he struck the rock, which of all rocks present was the best fitted to pour forth water. So it was split and water streamed out of it. And God made it into twelve fountains according to the number of tribes (Qur'ān II, 57/60).

And among the barbarians there was a man who studied the sciences of the prophets and knew their books by heart. He obeyed the devil and was out for worldly gain. And he advised his people to send prostitutes to the Israelites in order to increase fornication among them. Then the beneficent force (emanating from God) might disappear and divine providence might be lost[32] ... But Moses managed to drive away the prostitutes.

Then they fought the barbarians. And God granted victory to them over those areas and settled them there ... And Moses consolidated their unity. He taught them the Torah, admonished and purified them, and maintained law and order ...

Thus is God's dealing with His beloved worshippers : He makes life easy for them; He gives them great renown and renders them popular with the people. And if men jointly put themselves in God's hands and obey His commands without hesitation or embarrassment, God provides them with all the means of subsistence He is in possession of, and blesses their fields, cattle and earnings.

Among the subjects in which God instructed Moses was alchemy. Korah, a cousin of Moses, who also acquired some knowledge of it, had become very rich through it. He knew, however, no limits, violated moral standards and abode by no rule. He was of the kind of the Pharaohs. Moses called a halt to him, but he could not be restrained. He had a secret hate of Moses, and imputed intercourse with prostitutes to him. Then Moses earnestly invoked God against him, and God "caused the earth to swallow up him and his house" (Qur'ān, XXVIII, 81) ...

Moses held the belief that there was no man in the world more learned than himself. Therefore he no longer tried to acquire more knowledge. So God sought for an occasion to stimulate him to obtain more knowledge, as He also did in connection with our prophet, merely with the command : "Say, O Lord, increase me in knowledge!" (Qur'ān XX, 113/114) ...

Well then, one day Moses delivered an address in order

to inform the people of what God had told him. And this speech impressed the hearers to such a degree that their hearts were filled with wonder. And one of them asked him: "Can there be found anybody more learned than you?" He replied: "No, such a man I never met". Then God revealed: "Yes, such a man does exist. Our servant Khiḍr is more learned than you are", i.e. with regard to God's designs on certain occasions, on account of which he could function as an instrument for carrying His designs into execution—as on the other hand Moses was more learned with regard to provisions of the law and divine commandments to be observed by all men, on account of which he could function as an instrument for the consolidation of religious institutes. Then Moses inquired: "How can I find that person?" And by inspiration he was told that a salted fish would show him the way. But he did not hear in which way he would be taken to Khiḍr. Accordingly, Moses and his young servant Joshua set out in search of him. In a basket they carried with them some barley breads and a salted fish. And they had to keep moving till at long last they arrived at a rock. At that place Moses fell asleep because of the fatigues of the journey. Joshua squatted to perform the ritual ablution before prayer. Then some of the water dripped upon the fish, which restored it to life. And this was so, because water possesses the peculiar quality of restoring aquatic animals to life, and (on that occasion) a beneficent force was produced in that peculiar quality. Then the fish fell into the sea, and in its track a dry path (leading to the isle where Khiḍr lived) emerged. Thus by this token Moses and Joshua encountered Khiḍr.[33]

Now in the case of these two men before us, three events were shown to Moses by Khiḍr to illustrate the manner in which God may provide contrivances or reconditionings for the benefit of His creatures. Then God uses one of His servants as an instrument for the accomplishment of an intended operation.

(The fact of the matter is that) provisions of the law bear on universal principles and applications of jurisprudence, whereas contrivances bear on affairs conducive to a particular prudence, in accordance with which every decision is adjusted to the circumstances of the moment. All this is a most subtle knowledge, only known to him who has become an instrument of God. Then he comes to understand precisely the underlying idea of events like the three shown by Khiḍr.

Although with regard to legal provisions there was no better informed man than he, Moses could nevertheless not grasp that other knowledge (about the very purports of God's proceedings), as when he asked permission to look upon God, or when he apologized for having killed that Egyptian ... So it was part of God's wisdom to show some events to Moses (in order to acquaint him with that knowledge). Thus (when Moses and Khiḍr embarked in a ship,) the latter made (to the dismay of the former) a hole in it in order to prevent that a tyrant would seize it by force (and this was the actual purpose not apprehended by Moses) ... And (secondly) (again to the dismay of Moses) Khiḍr killed somebody, while there was not even question of blood-feud, only because of his being an unbeliever by nature. Would he (a youth) have remained alive, then (and that was in this case the actual reason of the action taken) this (unpleasant) disposition would have become apparent and he would have distressed his parents on account of his rebellion and unbelief. And God might give them as more virtuous child in exchange for him. (The third instance of irrational behaviour, witnessed by Moses was that Khiḍr repaired a wall without claiming recompense).

And he raised the wall (and now follows the particular prudency) to safeguard property which was entrusted to a righteous and beloved servant of God (and belonged to two orphaned youths) ...

After receiving Moses into His glory, God continued to supply the Israelites with good leaders. And He sent prophets to warn them, to announce good news to them, to further their spiritual life, to induce them to the good and to keep them from evil ... And among those prophets there were born leaders like Joshua, scholars like Isaiah, Elisha and Samuel, and austere ascetes like Elias. Decisive (for the choice of a particular type of prophet) were considerations of expediency and timeliness.

Prophets are sons of one man by different mothers : the father they have in common is the divine education preparing them for prophethood; the different mothers are their innate and acquired dispositions.

SAMUEL, DAVID, SOLOMON, JONAH

God has mentioned in the Torah that the Israelites would twice gain the victory, although they were working mischief and manifested unbelief, and that in both cases He would "incite against them servants of formidable bravery,[34] forcing their way through the countries. And when (the realization of) the promise of the first was to come" (Qur'ān XVII, 4 f.), they disobeyed the laws of the Torah. So God sent Goliath against them. Some of them he killed, others he made captive. And he stole the Ark, in which sacred relics left by the family of Moses and Aaron were kept (like the shoes and staff of Moses, and the mitre of Aaron). Thereupon they felt sorry and repented. They returned to their prophet Samuel and asked for a king, for they knew that fighting an enemy, great in number, would only be feasible in unity, and (under the command of) a man who applied himself to the welfare of the nation ... And God prompted the believers to the Holy War. He strengthened their hearts, emboldened them, and gave them mastery over their enemies ...

In this story there occur several provisions from God. One of them was that when Saul became a king and they held against him that he had no predecessors and no abundance of wealth, the prophet Samuel allayed their suspicions that there would be no use in obeying what God by inspiration had arranged for His creatures. Accordingly, God produced a sign (of his kingship) as a reassurance to them, to wit the return of the Ark with the relics left by the family of Moses and Aaron, borne by the angels (Qur'ān II, 248 f./247 f.). This happened in the following way : when the enemies began to suffer from calamities like want of rain, and quarrels among themselves, the angels suggested to them that all this was owing to the presence of the Ark. Consequently, they dragged it from one town to the other till in the end they came in the neighbourhood of the Israelites. They transported it on a cart and directed it to the Israelites to harm them. In fact, however, it was a contrivance to the Israelites' advantage. And when the Ark reached the Israelites without needing any effort on their part, it was indeed to them a sign (of Saul's kingship). And scenting the relics of Moses and Aaron they felt the presence of God; peace of mind descended upon them. Now they could acknowledge that he was a king, supported and blessed by an unseen world.

A second provision (from God) had to do with Saul's problem of finding out the state of affairs in his army, the degree of bravery and the mental attitude of the soldiers, in order to know to what extent he could rely on each of them. He was at a loss how to set about this, since he was in a hurry and this was something which could only be managed by a time-wasting trial. So God showed him a river by which they could be tested. Saul forbade them to taste of its water, except as much of it as filled the hand (Qur'ān II, 249/250). Thus firmness of character, mental strenghth and continence would be disclosed ...

A third provision (from God) was that when God wanted to give David great renown among the Israelites and to make him king, He caused a stone to speak; i.e. when David would pass by it God would reveal its function; it would seem to him that he heard the stone say that it would be the instrument to kill Goliath. (At the same time) He brought Saul into a state of agitation, so that he pledged himself to give the killer of Goliath half of the kingdom and his daughter as bride. Then He heartened David, made him to stretch out his hand (which held the stone) in the direction of Goliath's nostrils, and then commanded the wind to carry the stone straight to them. By this arrangement He caused Goliath to die. And the support He wanted to lend to the Israelites He realized by driving away the unbelievers, and by raising the status of David by making him king.

David was a brave and strong personality and was possessed of exceptional governing talents. Therefore He made him a delegate on earth, conferred on him the dignity of *imām* (head of the community), put the Israelites under his charge and imposed on them obligations to him ... So in a proper manner he carried on the government of them ... And he established harmony between the Israelite tribes.

Impressive was the way in which David worshipped God

and humbled himself before Him. Therefore God inspired him with psalms, 150 in total. Every psalm contains a prayer, an earnest supplication, a craving for blessing in this life and the hereafter, or a taking refuge with God.

And he was also endowed with manual dexterity. Therefore he was inspired with the art of making coats of mail so that he could make a good living for himself and so that he could shield other people from danger (Qur'ān XXI, 80).

And God made the recital (of the Holy Scripture) easy for him, so that he could recite in a certain space of time more (verses) than anybody else. And this was because God had extended a beneficent force to his tongue and intellect. Thus he could clearly remember every word in a little while. And he acquired quickly the correct pronunciation (of the words in the Holy Scripture). And God endowed him with a beautiful voice by which he made a deep impression on men and animals. He also subjected the mountains to him, so that when he glorified the Lord they responded to him (by their echo) in the evening and at sunrise (Qur'ān XXXVIII, 17/18). This was like a boom returning when a shout is raised in a vault ...

David also had peculiar experiences. One of them was that his eye fell on a handsome woman, and he came to love her fervently. He was of a sensual nature and attractive to women because of his hot temperament. But his desire to marry her was an infringement of good morals. And he refused to observe the law which did not allow this. So God pointed this out to him by showing him two angels who litigated with each other. One of them said : "Now this my brother had ninety and nine ewes, and I had but a single ewe; and he said : make me her keeper; (but he has not given it back) and he has bullied me into it by his words" (Qur'ān XXXVIII,

22/23). In this way David was confronted with his delict by a symbolical form of it. And God was greatly incensed against him. David understood that this had been a dream to call his attention to the crime he had perpetrated. Accordingly, he asked God's forgiveness, turned repentantly to Him, and continued with atonements till he was forgiven ...

Another of those peculiar experiences was that when he asked God for a child to succeed him, God answered his prayer and granted him Solomon, who was intelligent, religious, wise, and of an unblemished character. He became a partner of David in the adjudication of intricate legal cases; and in particular situations he readily recognized the most correct and appropriate solution. Thus one night some people's sheep had strayed into a field (of somebody else), and this case was brought before David. And he pronounced a verdict in accordance with what is stated (in general) in the chapter of the law concerning damage. In this case, however, there was the particular issue of an injury suffered by a cattle-keeper. And God gave Solomon to understand what in this particular situation was the most correct and appropriate solution (Qur'ān XXI, 78 f.).[35] In cases of a similar nature Solomon pronounced a great many verdicts.

Solomon also received knowledge about the second and third stages of man's social evolution (*irtifāq*). And David appointed him as successor to the throne.

And Solomon was taught the speech of birds (Qur'ān XXVII, 16) ... Birds (as you should be aware of) possess different voices connected to the (different) emotions they experience, such as anger, fright, lust or hunger ... And God may impart even to mystics some knowledge of the speech of birds ...

And God made the wind and *djinns* (nymphs and satyrs of

the desert) subservient to Solomon (Qur'ān XXI, 81 f.). The point of this is that fundamentally wind, fire etc. derive their existence from the divine vivifying power (*qayyūmiyya*) extant in water, the prime element ... Perfect worshippers are sometimes closely related to vivifying powers (which have specific manifestations, such as in one case air, in another fire, etc.). Thus Solomon had a close affinity with the vivifying forces producing wind and fire,[36] and he was in the possession of a strong willpower to make objects subservient (to himself). When through that affinity more force was added to his willpower he made (even) devils subservient, to build for him "whatever he pleased, of sanctuaries, and images" (Qur'ān XXXIV, 12/13), and "to dive into the sea (to get pearls for him), and to do other works beside that" (Qur'ān XXI, 82). And sitting on his throne he gave orders to the wind, and it transported the throne in any direction he wished.

Also Solomon had peculiar experiences. One of them was that once horses were shown to him which aroused his admiration. And he was taken up with them to such an extent that he forgot the hour of prayer. But (when he perceived his omission) he was greatly concerned about it, so that he killed or hamstrung them (cf. Qur'ān XXXVIII, 30 f./31 f.).

A second peculiar experience was that when he was annoyed at the little inclination of his chiefs to wage war, he desired to have sexual intercourse with his wives in order that each of them would give birth to a hero who could fight for God's cause. Thus he relied on the processes of causality and forgot to trust in God and to call for His help.—Somebody who has the knowledge of Truth, however, does not rely on the processes of causality until he has first called for God's help and until he perceives that in those processes there is an influx of a (divine) design.—And God informed him about this by means of a complete lack of fertility of his wives. On account of his frequent cohabitations his seminal fluid had become thin, and the only result he gained was (a son with) a deformed body. And that hunch-backed body was placed on his throne. Then he understood the underlying idea (of that event), and turned to God in repentance. He asked Him for help for his kingship, saying: "O my Lord, pardon me and grant me a kingship that nobody after me will be worthy of" (Qur'ān XXXVIII, 33 f./34 f.).

A third peculiar experience was that (one day) he passed the valley of ants 'on the back' of the wind (which carried his throne). "There an ant said: " O ants, go into your dwellings, that Solomon and his armies may not crush you" (Qur'ān XXVII, 18). And she took measures of precaution as far as her knowledge permitted. Solomon heard her and understood her words. And he was thankful for the acquired knowledge of the language of beasts.

A fourth peculiar experience was that (one day) during a review of the birds the hoopoe was missing. Solomon threatened it dreadfully (with severe torments). Then God notified him of a remarkable account[37] that was a mercy for the hoopoe, since (owing to it) it was saved from (Solomon's) threats and a mercy for Solomon, since (because of it) the reign of the queen of Sheba would fall into his hands, and a mercy for the queen of Sheba and her people, since they (now) would find the (true) faith. Thus at that time thanks to the (divine) wisdom Solomon was acquainted with the true condition of the queen of Sheba through the hoopoe. And the latter referred to her paganism, wealth and beauty (cf. Qur'ān XXVII, 23 f.) ...

A final peculiar experience was that God withdrew the throne of the queen of Sheba from the law of gravitation and invested it with properties of the *'ālam al-mithāl* (so that it could be easily transported through the air[38]) ... Next, Solomon devised ruses to test the intelligence of the queen and to examine her beauty, for he desired to marry her. So he disguised (for her) her throne, but still she recognized it. And he saw her legs (when she, mistaking the polished floor for a pool of water, lifted up her robes to pass through it), and he noticed that she was a most beautiful woman (Qur'ān XXVII, 41f., 44) ...

The dynasty of David remained on the throne without a break. Sometimes a king of distant countries overpowered the Israelites, but then God revealed to their prophets a promise of efficient aid. And thereupon He provided a wonderful contrivance to give them such efficient aid ... Thus centuries passed by.

Next, there was in Nineveh a people exceeding the proper bounds (of morality) and violating (ethical standards). So God in His wisdom ordered Isaiah, the prophet of that time, to warn them (against God's doom) preferably through one of his own followers. Accordingly, he sent Jonah. The reason why Isaiah chose Jonah was that the latter owed his existence to God's generosity and providence. For he was begotten in a miraculous way, his parents being of advanced age (at that moment). He was surrounded by (divine) solicitude, and in his childhood God took his charge upon Himself by inspiring tame and untamed animals to suckle him. Further, He procured him a wife by showing him in a dream whose daughter's hand he should ask for in marriage and by showing that person (in a dream) to whom he should give his daughter in marriage.

All in all, Jonah was a true object of divine solicitude, and on this account Isaiah chose him for that mission. He, however, recoiled from the struggle against a brutish people; and the command of the prophet (Isaiah) evoked in him an emotional and mental reluctance. This brought serious discredit upon him. So God punished him : his wife was lost, one of his two sons found a watery grave and the other one was devoured by a wolf. Thus he suffered, and he turned to God in repentance. He gave up a life of comfort and took up the hardships of missionary work.

When he came to the Ninevites, he called them to belief in God's Unity. But they gave him the lie and apprehended and molested him. Fervently he invoked God (imploring Him) for their doom. But the time was not yet ripe for it, since God does not approve of the doom of a people until His curse of them has become final ...

Then Jonah witnessed some (extraordinary) events. One of them was that when the people (of Nineveh) foresaw their doom[39] and turned to God in repentance, abasing themselves before Him, God forgave them and revoked the doom (Qur'ān X, 98). The devil (however) argued Jonah into the fatal thought that (by the passing by of the judgment which he had threatened them with) he had been made a liar and the people (now) were determined to abuse him. So he became frightened of them and fled from them without abasing himself before God, in spite of the fact that putting their affairs into the hands of God is actually incumbent on prophets ... He boarded a ship. A gale sprang up. "And lots were cast, and the lot fell against him". Consequently, he was thrown into the sea, "and a fish swallowed him". Then "he glorified God", and expiated his sins. God forgave him and divine mercy became his share. The fish vomited him up "upon the bare shore, while he was sick. And a gourd tree grew up over him" (Qur'ān XXXVII, 141-146), so that he would not be annoyed by flies. And the idea of feeding him with their milk suggested itself to untamed animals, as it seemed to them that he was one of their young. In their hearts a similar mercy arose as they felt for their young. Thus God took full charge of him, so that he regained strength and health. After that the gourd tree withered and the female gazelle (who had fed him) went away. And he grieved over them. Then God said to him by revelation: "O Jonah, you weep over a gourd tree which you have not watered, and over a female gazelle whom you have not provided with the means of subsistence; and you do not weep over the hundred thousand, or even more (Ninevites)!" ...

Next, Jonah passed people who had kept their gathered fruits in the field. So he remarked to them: "Why do you leave your fruits to rot, and are you not concerned about them?" Then God said to him by revelation: "O Jonah, you are concerned about the fruits of these people, and not about the hundred thousand, or even more!"

Next, he received the hospitality of a potter. Then God said to him by revelation that he should tell the potter to break his pottery. Thereupon the man abused him, shouting: "I see you are crazy!" Thus by such an instance God showed him (the absurdity of) the designs he had on the people entrusted to him ... Then he abased himself before God and turned to Him in repentance. And God forgave him on account of his sincere repentance and took charge of him as before. And He brought back to him his wife, granted him a hundred dinars, and brought back to him his sons ... And He gave him great renown among his people.

And this is because God is like a mirror, as He has said: "Only your own deeds I reckon against you". If somebody has gained a beautiful colour (by his doings) he will be richly rewarded (by God who 'mirrors' his colour); and if he has gained a bad colour, he will be badly remunerated. Men's hearts lie in the fingers of the Merciful. If He entertains malevolent designs upon somebody, He turns the hearts (of other people) towards mistreating him; and if He intends the well-being of somebody, He turns the hearts (of other people) towards being beneficial to him. This is the standing pattern of God's behaviour, in particular with regard to men who devote themselves exclusively to God's cause and of whose education He has taken charge. Amongst them was Jonah.

ZACHARIAH, MARY, JOHN THE BAPTIST AND JESUS

Anne was barren and advanced in years. But on viewing a dove feed her young she became very desirous of issue. And weeping she prayed to God. Then God extended His beneficent power to that viewing and eagerness (of her). So He removed her sterility and restored to her her courses. This is in accordance with the accounts of physicians (stating) that on viewing a copulation of animals fresh energy is given to the reproductive organs, because of which an impotent man may regain sexual power. Likewise on viewing a dove feed her young ones she came to think of child-bearing and to hanker for it. Thus her imperfection healed.

Next, a longing for a male child arose in her heart. Thus her imagination, firm resolution and expectation exercised an influence upon the fetus. Consequently, Mary was born blessed with a virile disposition. And as in the case with great personalities, she gained a strong body, a harmonious temperament, a sensitive religiousness and a fine purity. Therefore the Prophet has said: "Many men have been perfect, (but among women only Mary, the daughter of 'Imrān, and Āsiya, the wife of the Pharaoh,[40] were perfect; and 'Ā'isha's[41] superiority over women is like the superiority of *tharīd*[42] over other kinds of food"). Mary was a woman with the qualities of a man, as there are also men with an effeminate nature. And this was because by nature she looked out for God and centred all her hopes in Him ...

And when Anne had brought her forth as a female, she felt painfully affected before God, since only boys could be consecrated to His service. But God accepted Mary's being consecrated to His service, because she was a woman blessed with the qualities of a man. And He induced Zachariah and the other custodians of the temple to accept her, though it was contrary to the custom (Qur'ān III, 31 f./36 f.).

One of the provisions of divine providence for Mary was that He considered Zachariah as the only person to whose care she should be committed, inasmuch as he was a prophet, a scribe, and full of affection for her, while his wife was her maternal aunt. But since each of the custodians of the temple and the scribes held that he should have control of her education, He induced them to get the dispute decided "by casting their reeds" into the river (Jordan) (Qur'ān III, 39/44). In this was implied the (divine) contrivance to show that Zachariah was within his rights (in acting as her guardian).

Another provision of divine providence was that He showed miracles to Mary, by creating fruits for her (merely) by saying : "Be !" without the process of causality being required, in the same way as things are created by God for the inhabitants of Paradise (Qur'ān III, 32/37). And Zachariah possessed knowledge of divine mysteries and was acquainted with God's customary procedure in His creation. So he knew that in those days wonderful phenomena produced by spiritual energies could be expected, and that at that time an act of creation would not have to depend on a process of causality, as was also the case with the creation of Adam. So he begged of God a son, who would later succeed him to maintain the office of scribe and to exhort people to obedience to God, for he was afraid that his cousins on his father's side[44] (who were very wicked men) would run after wordly gain (when occupying this office), so that they would go astray and lead astray. Accordingly, he implored (God) fervently. God answered his prayer, rejuvenated him and removed the sterility of his wife. Thus John (the Baptist) was born, wise and devoted to God. He had no sexual intercourse with women; for all that which is brought into being without earthly processes of causality[45] displays little affinity to bestial qualities.[46] He was deprived of worldly comfort, but blessed with all that pertains to ways of worshipping God. John and Jesus were given to asceticism. They liked anonymity, and kept aloof of (political) leadership and of worldly delights. It is so because human perfections manifest themselves in an individual only in so far as his nature has an aptitude for them. If he be intelligent, his perfections consist of sagacity and accomplished scholarship. And if he have a natural disposition for impartiality and prudence in the conduct of affairs, dominion will be allotted to him—if he turns to God—.

When Zachariah asked for a sign that his wife would become pregnant of a son who would be a bearer of good news, God said to him by revelation : "You shall not speak to men for three days" (Qur'ān III, 36/41). And this was because as soon as God's solicitude and the willpowers of the *al-mala al-a'lā* descended upon earth and were directed towards him, an angelic atmosphere surrounded his soul, on account of which he could not speak to men except by vague signs.

Next, in the days that spiritual energies poured down upon that site (i.e. the temple of Jerusalem) her courses came upon

Mary. As soon as she was clean she retired from the people to a distant place to wash herself, and she let down a screen and took off her clothes. Then God sent her Gabriel in the shape of a well-built, vigorous and good-looking young man. Thereupon Mary, herself of a strong constitution, saw him. Fearing that he would harm her, she turned to God that He might defend her. Then she had a wonderful experience (Qur'ān XIX, 16 ff.). In her body there was a sudden rising of the functions of reproduction as during a cohabitation, and as sometimes the mere sight (of a charming lady) brings on an ejaculation of sperm. Her soul found refuge with God and protection by Him, so that it was filled with the experience of being guarded by the unseen world. And as regards her human individuality, that had the great honour of having commerce with the Faithful Spirit (i.e. Gabriel).

And when Gabriel said : "I am only a messenger of your Lord (having come) to give you a pure boy" (Qur'ān XIX, 19), she rejoiced, was happy, and at ease. When Gabriel ascertained this state of her mind, he blew upon her vulva. The blow titillated her womb and thus it caused the conception. Her seminal fluid obtained the power of the seminal fluid of a man. So she became pregnant. All the characteristics of Mary prevailing at that moment, such as her loyalty to God and her taking refuge with Him, and her being rejoiced and gladdened by an angelic atmosphere, where laid in the fetus ... Simultaneously, the condition of the *ālam al-mithāl* and the specific qualtities of the spirit were laid down in it by the blowing of Gabriel, i.e. the actual creative cause. Accordingly, its nature received a strength and insight like that of Gabriel. Ensuing from this was God's strengthening Jesus with the Holy Spirit (as is stated in Qur'ān II, 81/87; 245/253; V, 109/110).

When Mary had given birth (to Jesus), God showed her wonderful signs. One of them was that the angels announced all the perfections which God would bestow on her son. And to her were indicated all the spiritual experiences and perfections he would master during his childhood, his adolescence and his prime of life (Qur'ān III, 40 f./ 45 f.).

A second wonderful sign was that when (during the birth of the child) she resorted to a withered date palm, new life began to stream into it and within a little while it regained its green colour and supplied (her) with fruits. Also God caused a spring to gush forth for her (Qur'ān XIX, 24 f.).

And a third wonderful sign was that when she was accused of fornication, God removed the false accusation by putting words (of exoneration) into the mouth of the infant (Jesus) (Qur'ān XIX, 28 ff./27), though being at an age in which children as yet cannot speak.

When Jesus became a young man, knowledge, the Book (containing the Gospel) and sagacity were granted to him without the need of instruction, for spiritual power was laid in him. Wonderful signs were seen appearing through him. Thus he advised the people what they should eat and what they should store up in their houses (Qur'ān III, 43 b/49 b);[47] and he made of clay, the figure of a bird, breathed into it, and it became a bird by the leave of God (Qur'ān III, 43a/49a). Along with the diffusion of his breath into the clay, life streamed into the figure of the bird ... After that, if fell dead.

And he revived the dead, by the leave of God, for one's soul, though incapable of putting life into the body, can produce psychic effects upon it. Because of Jesus' prayer God extended beneficent power to that soul, and through this life was reflected (upon the dead body). Thus the dead regained life. But then he died again as soon as Jesus departed from him.

Jesus' system of belief showed liberalism and flexibility. And he made lawful for the Jews some of those things which were prohibited to them (Qur'ān III, 44/50). And this could be done because rigid laws[48] had been enacted only at the time that there obtained in them a collision of the angelic with the bestial.

Jesus was, so to say, an angel walking on earth. The Jews charged him with heresy, and conspired to kill him. "They plotted, but God plotted too; and God is the best of plotters" (Qur'ān VIII, 30).

Therefore God gave him a shape made of material of the *'ālam al-mithāl*, took him up into heaven and lent his likeness to a disciple or an enemy of his. And that man they killed, being under the impression that he was Jesus (Qur'ān IV. 156/157). Next, God aided his disciples against their enemies, so they did prove victorious (Qur'ān LXI, 14).

MOHAMMED

There are (various) circumstances that explain the sources from which our Prophet derived all kinds of knowledge :

a) there was a natural affinity between him and the *al-mala al-a'lā* ... For that reason his heart was continually strengthened by them, at one time by their manifesting themselves to him (while he was awake), at another time by their speaking to him and giving inspirations into his heart, and a third time by his vision of them in a dream ... And on account of this bond (between him and them) his determination used to be adjusted to their will, and all the time, whether he was engaged in a Holy War or withdrawn to his mosque, he was encompassed by their blessings ... Similarly, it was also on account of this bond that his breast was split and filled with wisdom and faith[49] and that he was transported by night to the temple of Jerusalem, then to the heavens and so on ...

b) thanks to the disposition which God had endowed on him, he was entitled to obtain from the *al-mala al-aʻlā* the knowledge of the way to refine his soul ...

c) God gave him intelligence by which he could find out the proper means to institute a healthy society (*irtifāqāt*), such as good breeding, domestic economy, social intercourse, civic economy and the management of the community ...

d) among the favours of God to His servants there was His desire to make a spring of mercy flow for mankind, benefiting Arabs and non-Arabs alike ... And this was because both of them had given themselves up to evil practices ... Consequently, it was a favour to them that now their attention was drawn to the pernicious conditions into which they had got themselves and they were shown the way to God ...

e) his sanctified soul was prepared for receiving revelations about past and future events in the world ... And after having been entrusted with world-dominion and the charge of the community, it was essential—while it participated (in this way) in the great policies of the *al-mala al-aʻlā*—that his soul would hold reflections of stories of bygone generations and of events concerning the society as a whole, pertinent one way or an other to the well-being or ruin of the community itself, ... and likewise of events regarding the Resurrection, as e.g. the appearance of the Anti-Christ, the arrival of the Mahdî,[50] the descent of Jesus, and of 'the animal of the earth' ...

You should know that the Prophet did not allow us[51] to speculate about (God's) Being, rather he forbade us to do so by saying: "Don't speculate about the Creator" ... Within this prohibition come also the discussions about the divine Attributes, i.e. the explanations of the true nature of God's Attributes ... The Prophet discussed merely subjects which Arabs and non-Arabs could grasp, and only for the sake of their praise and glorification of the Lord he applied divine Attributes ...

One category of miracles (performed by Mohammed), handed down by word of mouth, consisted of this that a lot of beneficent force was often extended to his prayer for food or drink, in which case either the profit of it or the quantity of it was increased ... This is a quality which the Prophet shared with the *mufahhamūn*[52] and saints ...

A second category of miracles consisted of most uncommon occurrences brought about by causes of great rarity. On this account they were called 'preternatural phenomena'. In fact everything that is called a 'preternatural pheneomenon' is a common occurrence, but ... wheresoever things happen which the general public have not anticipated there is talk of preternatural phenomena. Sometimes that which the general public considers to be a common occurence actually is much more wonderful ... And sometimes a quality unusual for one species is natural for another species, as with *djinns* far-reaching clairvoyance, traversing of the earth, the capacity of appearing under different forms and of secretly exercising influence upon somebody else are usual matters ...

Well then: if such (uncommon) occurrences take place as the prognostication of events or a punitive wonder as befell the 'Ādites and Thamūdites because of their disobedience, God makes of them 'preternatural phenomena' for a prophet for one reason or another ... To this kind of occurrences belongs the splitting of the moon,[53] being an extraordinary event which God caused to happen as a sign of the approaching Resurrection ... It is not necessary (to assume) that the moon had actually split in two. Rather there may have occurred something like a smoke, the swooping down of a star, an eclipse of the sun or of the moon which the people observed in the sky. In this case they applied to those phenomena in front of them Arabic terms which put into words the subjective impression they had received from them. And the Qur'ān has been revealed in the Arabic language. (Thus e.g.) 'Abd Allāh b. Mas'ūd—and it is enough to merely mention him[54]— reports: "They (i.e. the Qurayshites who opposed Mohammed) were hit by a drought. And when they looked up, they saw a smoke in the sky (as a fata morgana of a rain-cloud)". In that connection was revealed the passage: "... the day when the heaven brings a manifest smoke" (Qur'ān XLIV, 9/10).

Ibn al-Mādjishūn, an authority (on the Malikite rite of Islamic Law), has declared: "Not God will be transformed from one shape into another on the Day of Resurrection, but men will see Him in different shapes (since God will work changes in their organs of sight on that day)". And he has also stated: "This phenomenon (of the 'splitted' moon) was occasioned by a cohesion of small particles of water into, so to say, one plane. Behind it there was a mountain or a dense cloud. Together these produced the effect of a mirror. When the moon was reflected in it, people observed two moons in the sky. And in the case that a part of the reflected and a part of the real moon were concealed, two halves were seen in the sky ..."

This theory, which I (sc. Shāh Walī Allāh) have just mentioned, according to me is possible and conceivable ...

But (only) God is the One who knows (the actual facts) ...

(To sum up :) All that pertained to the Prophet's way of life, his course of conduct and his adventures was the beneficial outcome of his being of a perfect harmony and of being supported by the *ḥazīra al-quds*. Therefore he distinguished himself in many respects as compared with his congeners. This is the last statement we wanted to make in this treatise. Praise be to God, the Lord of the inhabitants of the universe; God is sufficient for me and He is an excellent protector; God bless our chief Mohammed, his family and all his companions.

NOTES

¹ Refers to the episode when, as is told, Gabriel and Michael opened his breast and purified his interior parts in order to qualify him for his prophetic career.

² Presumably the author hints here at the episode, recorded in the Koran, in which is told that God taught Adam the names of all things, and since the angels did not know the names Adam instructed them.

³ This refers to the conception of an earth consisting of seven strata with spaces between them. In the first space are found human beings, in the second the winds, in the sixth the inhabitants of hell, in the seventh Satan.

⁴ Only twice did the Prophet see Gabriel in his true colours, i.e. with 600 wings. As a rule he appeared in the shape of Diḥya al-Kalbī, one of Mohammed's companions.

⁵ Direction into which the Muslims turn when praying toward the Kaʿba of Mecca.

⁶ After Adam who stayed on earth, it is now the turn of the angels who abide in the supermundane world of the ʿālam al-mithāl.

⁷ This dialogue, recorded in Qurʾān VII, 171/2, is said to bear upon a covenant which God made with mankind, when only pre-existent, after having taken from Adam's loins his whole posterity (as is the version in the traditions), or after their pre-figuration in the ʿālam al-mithāl (as is asserted here by this Indian mystic).

⁸ The two earliest of the five 'Arab' prophets mentioned in the Qurʾān. Hūd was sent to the tribe called ʿĀd, which is said to have been a mighty and haughty nation immediately after the time of Noah. Ṣāliḥ was the messenger to Thamūd who lived in North-West Arabia. According to the legend, at the prayer of Ṣāliḥ a rock travailed and brought forth a she-camel. This miracle, however, conveyed too little conviction to most of the Thamūd to induce them to acknowledge God, and eventually they even killed the animal.

⁹ A geographical term, usually interpreted as meaning curved sand dunes.

¹⁰ According to the traditional account, actually three clouds appeared in the sky, one white, one red and one black. Being given the choice of one of the three by a voice from heaven, the black one was chosen, presumably because of the greedy consideration that it would be laden with the most rain. The result was fatal, as precisely this one turned out to be fraught with divine vengeance.

¹¹ The Christian legend of the men, called in the Qurʾān (XVIII, 9-26)

NOTES 63

"the people of the cave", refers to youths who, persecuted, fled into a cave, where they sank into a miraculous sleep for 309 years.

12 She was, as is claimed by Muslim commentators, a daughter of this king of Egypt.

13 For this expression see Qur'ān II, 246/5.

14 *Sc.* to find out whether Mohammed was ready to perform 50 prayers a day, as Abraham had proved willing to sacrifice his son; the boon in regard of Mohammed was the sufficiency of 5 prayers a day, and in regard of Abraham the substitutive sacrifice of a ram.

15 An allusion to the sudden appearance of a ram which had been brought out of paradise, as is claimed by rabbinic and Muslim tradition.

16 According to Qur'ān XXXVII, 101 Abraham was ordered in a vision to sacrifice his son.

17 According to Arab ideas to refuse food is a sign of hostility; they, however, did not touch it because as angels they did not require food.

18 In all probability the hesitations of the wife of Lot are referred to here.

19 Here Shāh Walī Allāh cleverly extends the meaning this term has in Qur'ān XII, 6 where it is mentioned as the gift typical of Joseph, the reader of dreams. As this monograph, which has this term as its title, is written with the view of exposing basic notions in the prophetic stories, the expression is given the more extended sense of 'explanation of (significative) events'.

20 According to the Muslim commentators the witness for the defense, mentioned in Qur'ān XII, 26, was a cousin of Zulaykha, being then a child in the cradle. A better known parallel is Jesus' speaking in the cradle to reprove Mary's cousin Joseph for his unjust suspicions of her.

21 In Qur'ān XII, 67 it is mentioned that Jacob advised his sons not to enter the city, where Joseph resided, by one and the same gate. It would be better to pass through different gates. If entering in a single group, such is the unuttered fear, they might be subject to the evil eye.

22 By his continual weeping for grief, as is suggested in Qur'ān XII, 84, Jacob had lost his eyesight.

23 The traditions tell us that at the moment Job wanted to snatch up the golden grasshopper he heard a heavenly voice asking: "Don't you have sufficient property?", whereupon he replied: "Who can say of Your mercy: enough!"

24 In explanation of the obscure passage in Qur'ān XXXVIII 43/44, Muslim commentators relate the story of Job's inconsiderately taking an oath; the verse is often quoted as authorising any similar manner of release from hasty oaths.

[25] Whether and how far this Qur'ānic prophet can be identified with the Biblical Jethro is a matter of dispute.

[26] This is a statement of Mohammed, recorded in a tradition regarding a combatant who, badly wounded in the battle of Khaybar, committed suicide.

[27] Originally, as is told by Muslim Qur'ān commentators, it came from a myrtle of Eden.

[28] For it was in their own field that Moses beat the magicians.

[29] Notice that here again we have a clear instance of Shāh Walī Allāh's efforts of de-mythologizing prophetic stories, for according to the Qur'ān too (XXVI, 63) the cleavage of the sea was caused by a miraculous blow of Moses' staff, of which no mention is made in this exposition.

[30] By the Qur'ān the initiative of making the Golden Calf is attributed to this man, whose proper name is not recorded, instead of to Aaron.

[31] This must refer to Qur'ān II, 51/54, where Moses in saying : "O my people, you have done harm to yourselves by taking the calf (for a god). Therefore, turn to your Creator (in repentance) and slay one another (sc. the guilty among you)!"

[32] This story, recorded by the Muslim historian al-Ṭabarî, about Balaam's advising the Moabites to weaken the Israelite army by the offer of harlots, is of Talmudic origin.

[33] A legendary personage who is identified with the prophet Elias, the hero Gilgamesh and a cook of Alexander the Great, and who was rendered immortal and supernaturally wise by having found and drunk of the water of life, which in our story is sprinkled on the salted fish. Up to this point Shāh Walī Allāh has related the legend Muslim commentators produce in elucidation of and as a preliminary to the Qur'ānic passage of XVIII, 59/60-81/82. After this he will set forth the hidden rightful purposes of three incidents which at first sight seem of a criminal nature.

[34] Possibly Goliath and the Assyrian Sennacherib are alluded to here.

[35] David, as the Muslim exegetes explain, had pronounced the judgment that the owner of the field should take all the sheep in compensation for the damage, but Solomon, who was only eleven years old at the time, proposed the sensible amendment that the complainant should enjoy the profit of the sheep, that is their wool, milk, and lambs until the injury was repaired. And this proposal was approved by his father.

[36] *Djinns* are created of 'a smokeless flame' (Qur'ān LV, 14).

[37] This account, reported by the hoopoe which had returned meanwhile, concerned particulars about the queen of Sheba, which the bird had heard on a trip to the South, when it was sent out by Solomon to carry a message.

38 According to Qur'ān XXVII, 39, it was a *djinn* who took care of its transport to Solomon's palace: this happened without the knowledge of the queen herself.

39 For they found, as is reported by the Muslim Qur'ān-commentators, the heavens overcast with a black cloud, which shot forth fire, and filled the air with smoke.

40 Muslim commentators of the Qur'ānic verse LXVI, 11 in which she is mentioned, relate that she endured many cruelties at the hands of the Pharaoh because she believed in Moses.

41 The favourite wife of Mohammed.

42 A dish made of bread crumbs moistened with (meat-) stock, seasoned with garlic and mint.

43 All the reeds sank except that of Zachariah; and this was the token that the charge of Mary was to devolve on him.

44 See Zachariah's statement in Qur'ān XIX, 5 : "But I fear my kindred after my death".

45 An allusion to John's miraculous generation.

46 An allusion to the sensuality of man.

47 Here the Qur'ān seems to refer to what is recorded in passages like St. Matthew VI, 16-26.

48 Several prohibitory regulations concerning food were, as the Qur'ān argues, imposed on the Jews by way of punishment. See e.g. IV, 158/160 : "And for the iniquity of those who are Jews We have forbidden them goodly viands which had been allowed them before".

49 This refers to a sort of vocational vision in which angels were observed removing the black clot of sin out of Mohammed's breast and putting wisdom and faith in its place.

50 A saviour to appear shortly before the end of the world. A similar fuction the Muslims ascribe to Jesus, and sometimes also to 'the animal of the earth' (recorded in Qur'ān XXVII, 84/82) who is thought to be a person to lead the Muslim community into the right direction at the end of the world.

51 A concealed attack of Shāh Walī Allāh on the so-called *mutakallimūn*, the Muslim scholastics who are fond of holding subtle discourses on the relation between God's Being and Attributes.

52 i.e. people who are informed by the *al-mala al-aʻlā* and in whom, according to our author, elements of prophethood continue to exist, though in principle prophethood has been closed by Mohammed, the Seal of the Prophets.

53 Many Muslim scholars imagine the words ("the moon is split" in Qur'ān LIV, 1) to refer to a miracle God performed for Mohammed.

54 Being a famous companion of the Prophet.

GLOSSARY

ʿālam al-djabarūt — The divine Being reveals Itself on descending levels of differentiation. The lower the level, the greater the individuation and specification. These levels ane styled *ʿālams*, 'worlds'. Things in the *ʿālam al-djabarūt* are still in a state of superformal existence, in distinction to the lower *ʿālam al-mithāl*, where the objects possess subtle forms. The lowest level is the *nāsūt*, the world in which we live. At this point the evolution of individual forms has reached its fullest extent. The highest level is called *ʿālam al-lāhūt*. Here the divine Being is beyond any qualification, in contradistinction to the *ʿālam al-djabarūt*, the world below it, where the divine Being acquires 'names'.

ʿālam al-malakūt — An alternative term for the *ʿālam al-mithāl*.

ʿālam al-mithāl — This is the world of prefiguration, in which things and events are shaped before they are embodied in actual existence upon the earth, in the same way as an architect draws the shape of a house on a piece of paper before he builds it in the empiric reality. Its material is of a much more refined quality than that of our world, in which everything is composed of the four coarse elements: air, water, fire and earth. Accordingly having received a body of this fine and light material Jesus could ascend to heaven, and the throne of the Queen of Sheba could be transported through the air.

ḥanīfiyya — Before the time that monotheism had become a defined doctrine and an established institution, it was *ḥanīfiyya*, i.e. the religion in accordance with the natural disposition created in men by God (see Qurʾān XXX, 30). Thus it was the faith of people like Abraham, Joseph, and the parents of Moses.

ḥaẓīra al-quds — This is the site in the *ʿālam al-mithāl* where the decrees and provisions for men are determined, inasmuch as it is a luminous circle formed by the shining figures of the supreme angels convened to take decisions about the future of mankind.

imām of the species — According to the theory of creation of our author, after the coming into existence of the celestial spheres and elements, the *aʿyān* ('Ideas'), i.e. the archetypes (*imāms*) of the various species, appeared in the *ʿālam al-mithāl*. After that in the bodily world the human individuals, derived from the *imām* of the human species, came into being. Those archetypes are especially intent upon the preservation and welfare of the individuals appertaining to their species.

GLOSSARY

irtifāqāt — *Irtifāq* means literally 'to gain benefit by'. Our Delhi divine has coined of its feminine plural (*irtifāqāt*) a technical term denoting the ways and means people have at their disposal to raise cultural and social standards, while he qualifies the stages reached by their efforts to make a continuous progress simply as the first, second, third and fourth *irtifāq*, i.e. respectively the stages of nomadic life, urbanization, the establishment of polities, and supernationalism.

al-mala al-aʿlā — These are the supreme angels and the souls of departed prophets and other specifically qualified men, who inhabit the *ʿālam al-mithāl*.

al-nafs al-kulliyya — This represents the 'World Soul', which as a kind of *logos* directs everything in the universe.

al-ṭabīʿa al-kulliyya — This is actually the 'Universal Nature', which as the matrix of the cosmos encompasses all the mouldable materials of the universe.